# SEVEN BILLION AND COUNTING

## The CRISIS in GLOBAL POPULATION GROWTH

Michael M. Andregg

TWENTY-FIRST CENTURY BOOKS / MINNEAPOLIS

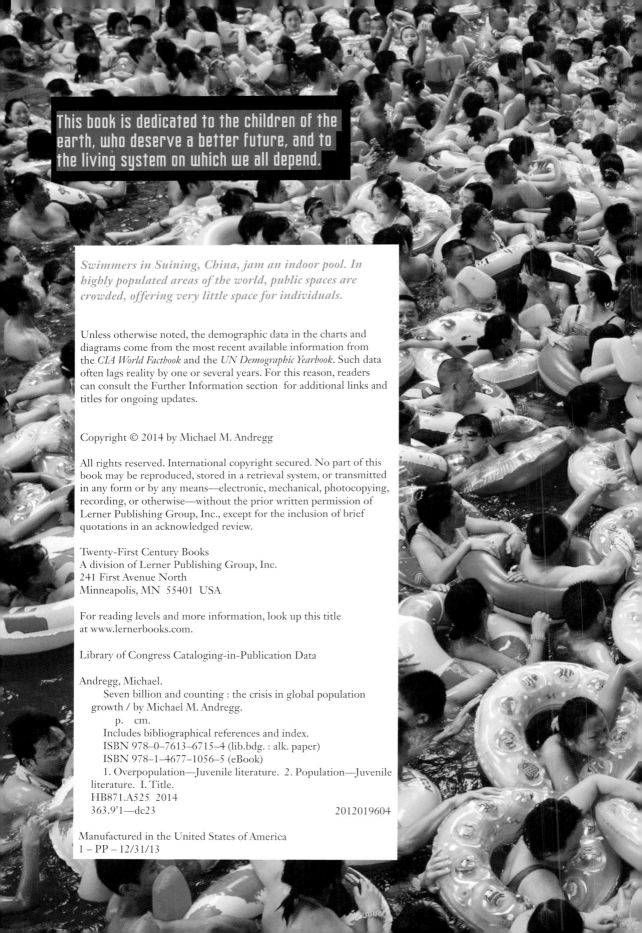

This book is dedicated to the children of the earth, who deserve a better future, and to the living system on which we all depend.

*Swimmers in Suining, China, jam an indoor pool. In highly populated areas of the world, public spaces are crowded, offering very little space for individuals.*

Unless otherwise noted, the demographic data in the charts and diagrams come from the most recent available information from the *CIA World Factbook* and the *UN Demographic Yearbook*. Such data often lags reality by one or several years. For this reason, readers can consult the Further Information section for additional links and titles for ongoing updates.

Twenty-First Century Books
A division of Lerner Publishing Group, Inc.
241 First Avenue North
Minneapolis, MN 55401 USA

For reading levels and more information, look up this title at www.lernerbooks.com.

Library of Congress Cataloging-in-Publication Data

Andregg, Michael.
    Seven billion and counting : the crisis in global population
growth / by Michael M. Andregg.
        p. cm.
    Includes bibliographical references and index.
    ISBN 978–0–7613–6715–4 (lib.bdg. : alk. paper)
    ISBN 978–1–4677–1056–5 (eBook)
    1. Overpopulation—Juvenile literature.  2. Population—Juvenile
literature.  I. Title.
HB871.A525 2014
363.9'1—dc23                                    2012019604

Manufactured in the United States of America
1 – PP – 12/31/13

# Contents

# INTRODUCTION

Whatever befalls the earth befalls the sons and daughters

of the earth. Men did not weave the web of life; we are merely one strand in it.

—*Chief Seattle (attribution disputed by some scholars), 1854*

Environmental degradation. Overcrowded cities. Urban jungles. Forced sterilization. One-child family policies. Resource wars. Extreme poverty. Hunger. Disease. Exploitation. Human misery. These are just some of the impacts of overpopulation as the planet's population tops seven billion human beings. At current rates of growth, experts suspect that Earth's human population may level off around ten billion people sometime in the twenty-first century. How did we get to this point, and is it sustainable?

Most experts say no. They point out that the living systems that sustain us are in trouble, which means we are in trouble too. This is why it matters whether Earth's population of seven billion plus continues to grow at rapid rates into the future. If we continue at this pace, the future of our planet may be very bleak indeed.

*Public transportation and other types of urban infrastructure do not always keep up with population pressure. Here, rush hour commuters overwhelm a train in Jakarta, Indonesia. The city has a population approaching ten million people.*

## STARTING AT THE BEGINNING

Human beings first emerged on Earth at least two hundred thousand years ago. The earliest groups of humans originated in Africa and eventually began to migrate into the Middle East and across Asia and Europe. Life was brutal. Death rates as a result of disease and misfortune (including harsh weather, starvation, and even being eaten by predators) were very high, and life expectancies were low.

Much more recently, about thirty thousand years ago, an ice age lowered the levels of the oceans. As one result, a natural land bridge linked what are now Russia and Alaska, allowing for a migration route into the Americas. During that time, the human population on Earth was probably not more than five million people. As humans around the world developed agriculture, cities and empires arose, some of them expanding across more than one continent. Since then, the global population has grown to more than seven billion people, about fourteen hundred times more than when Native Americans first came to the Americas.

Modern demographers (experts who study the statistics of human

*As large numbers of immigrants came to the United States in the nineteenth century, the population of urban areas exploded. For example, the population of New York City in 1800 was a little over 60,000 people. By the end of the century (below), the population had risen to 3.4 million.*

populations) estimate that the human population first reached one billion around 1804 CE. The early 1800s was a time of rapid industrial growth in Europe and the Americas. Cities and factories were booming. Agricultural science was developing as well, and farmers were able to dramatically increase their productivity to feed the growing numbers of people.

## Human Population Growth over Time

| HUMAN BEINGS (BILLIONS) | YEAR | YEARS TO ADD 1 BILLION PEOPLE |
|---|---|---|
| 7 | 2011 | 12 |
| 6 | 1999 | 12 |
| 5 | 1987 | 13 |
| 4 | 1974 | 14 |
| 3 | 1960 | 33 |
| 2 | 1927 | 123 |
| 1 | 1804 | 200,000 (approx.) |

While it had taken hundreds of thousands of years for the human population to reach one billion people, it took only 207 years to increase this number by six billion more humans. The strain this number of people puts on Earth's resources is enormous. People are planting crops in areas with poor soil in an effort to feed growing populations.

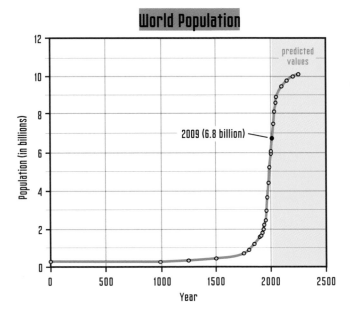

**World Population**

*This graph shows the rapid acceleration of Earth's human population. By the year 2000, the human population had reached six billion people, and we added another billion in the next twelve years. The graph also projects beyond current data, showing that human population may level off around ten billion people sometime in the twenty-first century. Experts feel this will likely happen through several mechanisms, including higher death rates in very poor countries and lower birth rates across the globe.*

Over time, this agricultural practice often leads to soil erosion or desertification. To make way for cities and farmland, humans have also been cutting down forests all around the world and are depleting carbon-based fuels such as oil and natural gas to fuel our cars, power our factories, and heat our homes. As a result of many things, including dependence on cars and other oil-burning vehicles, we are polluting Earth's waters, air, and land. This impacts the ability of animals and plants—many of which we depend upon for food, clothing, and building materials—to survive. Air pollution has also led to a rise in Earth's average temperature, leading to drought, severe storms, and rising sea levels across the planet.

The biggest ecological threat of all is species extinction. Experts estimate that we are already losing about one thousand species of plants and animals each year. This is a rate seen only five other times in geological history, including the period when dinosaurs died out.

*In arid regions of the world, the population explosion has led to overuse of land. Combined with climate change, these factors have increased the expansion of deserts. Saharan sand dunes in the western African nation of Mauritania, for example, are encroaching on urban areas such as that nation's capital city of Nouakchott (right).*

# CHAPTER 1
# DEMOGRAPHIC FUNDAMENTALS

There can be no permanent progress in

—*Norman Borlaug, the father of the Green Revolution, from his Nobel Peace Prize acceptance speech, Oslo, Norway, December 11, 1970*

Who actually counts all the people on our planet? Demographers do. They are the people who study demographics, the science of human statistics. Every government employs demographers, because human statistics are extremely important for setting public policies and for estimating the costs of public programs. To aid in these efforts, most governments count their populations every so often. For example, the United States conducts a census every ten years as mandated by the Constitution. The United Nations, an international peacekeeping organization, compiles population data from almost two hundred countries. Other sources for population data are the World Bank and the *CIA World Factbook*.

Schools, insurance companies, and medical organizations also rely on demographers. Professional demographers measure dozens of aspects of human populations. Among other tasks, they help to estimate how many schools will be necessary in the future or how much money will be available for retirement pensions. Basic demographics include eight measures, sometimes called variables. They are birth rates (BR), death rates (DR), growth rates (GR), life expectancies (LE), doubling times (dt), age distributions, migration, and equilibriums.

*Disease is one element that impacts a nation's death rate. For example, the HIV/AIDS epidemic has ravaged black communities in South Africa, which has the world's highest death rate. In this image, an HIV-positive woman* (wearing scarf) *chats with a volunteer caregiver and child.*

## BIRTH, DEATH, AND GROWTH RATES— AND WHY THEY MATTER

Birth rates refer to the number of children born per thousand people in a population in one year. Some demographers prefer a different measure called the total fertility rate, which estimates the number of children an average woman will have in her lifetime. It is a more complicated measure than that of how many babies are born each year in a population. Death rates are the number of people who die per thousand in a population in one year. In general, if birth rates are higher than death rates, a population grows. If birth rates are lower than death rates, the population declines in size.

Growth rates, usually expressed as a percentage, refer to the changes in a country's population size from year to year. If there is no migration into or out of a country, demographers calculate growth rates by subtracting death rates from birth rates. Human migration can have a big impact on actual growth rates. Therefore, the actual growth rate in a country is calculated by subtracting deaths from births and then adding (or subtracting) something called net international migration. Net migration is the sum of everyone entering a country on a long-term basis minus those who emigrate, leaving that country for the long term. All of these variables can be expressed in simple numbers, as percentages, or as rates per thousand per year.

Human populations in the twenty-first century vary from slightly negative growth rates in countries such as Russia and Japan to positive growth rates of 3 percent or even 4 percent in African countries

*A nurse rocks an infant in a maternity ward in Tokyo, Japan. That nation has a birth rate that is below replacement level. In other words, the birth rate there is lower than the death rate and the nation's population is in decline.*

such as Somalia and Burundi. Birth rates vary from a low of 7.7 per thousand in Singapore to a high of 50.1 per thousand in Niger, Africa. Arab countries of the Persian Gulf region such as Kuwait, the United

# The Middle East

The Middle East is not a continent. It is a region where three continents—Europe, Asia, and Africa—connect. It includes seventeen countries near Saudi Arabia and is a region of political and strategic importance. The five nations with the largest populations in the Middle East are (in descending order) Egypt, Iran, Turkey, Iraq, and Saudi Arabia. Saudi Arabia has about 27 million people as of 2013. It has a high birth rate of 19.0 and a very low death rate of 3.3 due to a very young population. The nation's population growth rate of 1.5 percent per year (dt = 47 years) and life expectancy of 74.6 years on average ranks among the highest among Middle Eastern nations.

In general, the nations of the Middle East—with the exception of Israel—are Muslim-majority countries. In these nations, use of birth control is much lower than in non-Muslim majority countries, leading to higher fertility rates and younger populations overall. Birth control is legal and available in most Muslim-majority countries, and many have government-supported family planning programs. However, the programs are fairly new, so shifts in reproductive practices within families do not match those in nations with family planning programs of much longer duration. Iran is an exception. Iranian women practice birth control at approximately the same rates as women in the United States.

# Norman Borlaug

Norman E. Borlaug *(below)* was born near Cresco, Iowa, on March 25, 1914. He received a PhD in plant pathology and genetics from the University of Minnesota in 1942. Known as the father of the Green Revolution, he helped to dramatically increase food production worldwide by developing high-yield, disease-resistant varieties of wheat and rice in agricultural research stations around the world. For this he received the Nobel Peace Prize in 1970. Proud of what he had accomplished, he also warned global agronomists that increasing food production alone was not enough to end world hunger. He recognized that without lower human birth rates, growth in the demand for food could outstrip all efforts to increase crop yields.

Arab Emirates, and Qatar have very young populations. For this reason, they have the lowest death rates on Earth at 2.0 per thousand. By contrast, the HIV/AIDS epidemic in South Africa has caused many premature deaths there, resulting in the world's highest death rate of 17.2 per thousand. In 2013 the United States had a birth rate of 13.7 per thousand, a death rate of 8.4 per thousand, and a growth rate of 0.9 percent.

In general, high birth and population growth rates are associated with low economic development such as in the African nations of Niger (GR = 3.63) and Zimbabwe (GR = 4.36). Nations such as Japan (GR = –0.08) and Germany (GR= –0.20), which are much more economically prosperous, tend to have much lower birth rates and population growth rates. This inverse trend is due to many factors. People in poor nations tend to have less access to nutritious food and receive poor medical care and education. Poor nations typically have no social security program or other national safety nets for elders, who therefore depend on surviving children to care for them. As a result, families often have more children to ensure that elders are looked after. Another critical factor is the degree to which women are freed from traditional social roles and constraints. In societies where women work outside the home and have access to medical care and education, women tend to have fewer children. Growth rates in those societies therefore tend to be lower than in countries where women are limited to the domestic sphere. The United States is closer to the middle on this statistic, with a growth rate for 2013 of about 0.9 percent.

## LIFE EXPECTANCY AND DOUBLING TIMES

Life expectancy is usually expressed as the number of years a baby can expect to live—on average—after birth. This statistic depends heavily upon the type of community into which a child is born. Each community has its own level of economics, technology, medicine, and other factors that influence the length of a person's life.

Countries such as the United States have long average life expectancies of 81.2 years for women and 76.2 for men. Japan has the highest, with 87.7 years life expectancy for women and 80.8 years for men. By contrast, poor countries such as Zambia and Mozambique in Africa have life expectancies for women of only 53.1 years, and 49.9 and 51.5 years for men, respectively. These numbers show that people in the world's poorest countries die much younger than people in the richest countries on Earth.

A doubling time (dt) is the number (in years) that demographers use to show how long it takes a population to double in size. This can be measured over time or predicted for the future using a formula that is based on a population's growth rate. For example, the human population on Earth doubled very quickly, from 1 billion to 2 billion people, in the years between 1804 and 1927. So for that period, the doubling time of the whole human population was 123 years. Then the population doubled from 2 billion people in 1927 to 4 billion people in 1974—a doubling time of only 47 years. If current trends continue, Earth will have 8 billion people around the year 2024. If so, the doubling time from 4 to 8 billion people will be about 50 years.

## Doubling Times and Growth Rates

| At 1% GR, dt = 70 years |
| At 2% GR, dt = 35 years |
| At 3% GR, dt = 23 years |

*These numbers show that at 1 percent growth rate per year, a population will double in about 70 years. At 2 percent growth, a population doubles in about 35 years. At 3 percent growth, doubling takes about 23 years. The math formula is dt = 70/GR%.*

Demographers can also determine doubling times by taking a mathematical constant called the natural logarithm of 2 (a number that is roughly .70) and dividing it by a population's growth rate in percent. This is commonly simplified as a math equation: dt = 70/GR%. The arithmetic of compound growth, in which population growth is linked to a rapid reduction in doubling times, is exactly the same as if you were calculating growth for a savings account or an investment that earns interest over time. In the financial scenarios, interest earnings

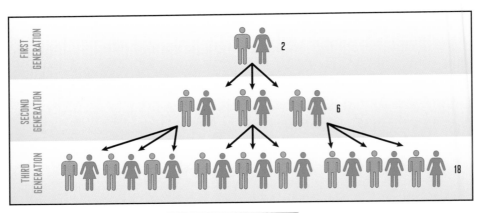

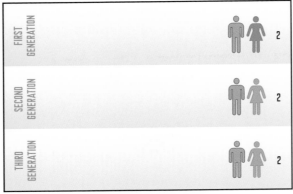

*The diagram above shows how quickly a population can grow over three generations through reproduction of just one couple. A sustainable planet requires a stable population, closer to the model at left, where each couple replaces itself but does not force the whole population to grow rapidly.*

increase more rapidly as the money in the account—from interest and from your deposits—grows. At 7 percent interest, your money would double in about ten years (70/7 = 10 years). Human populations do not grow that fast, however, and food production cannot grow that fast either.

## AGE DISTRIBUTIONS

Age distributions record a population by age categories. For example, a small human population such as that of an island village in the South Pacific might have one hundred people total. The age distribution would list these hundred people by age in groups of about ten years. So that village's one hundred people might be distributed like this: twenty children between zero and ten years of age, sixteen between ten and twenty years of age, the fourteen islanders who are between twenty and thirty years old, and so forth. Age distributions typically show men and women on opposite sides of a chart.

Age distributions are very important for calculating the long-term costs of government programs. For example, if a country has many young people but few elders, it will likely spend more money on schools than on health care for seniors. Fifty years later, when the country's former young people have become elders who need more health care, the situation may reverse. The country may then spend less on schools and more on health care, especially if birth rates and growth rates have declined over time, as often occurs with economic development.

Age distributions associated with high birth rates look quite different from age distributions associated with low birth rates. In chart form, the former look like pyramids, with more young people following each generation of elders.

Age distribution charts for developed nations, which tend to have low birth rates, look more like columns with pointy tops. Each age cohort (group) has similar numbers until the elders begin to die of old age, with few living past one hundred years of age. Countries with high birth rates develop a momentum of growth because there are more young people each year entering childbearing ages. It can take fifty years to work this momentum through the age distribution of a human population to the point where each age category (except the elders) has roughly the same number of people.

# Columnar Age Distribution: The USA, 2012

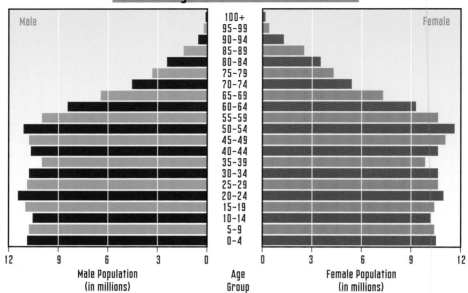

# Pyramidal Age Distribution: Niger, Africa, 2012

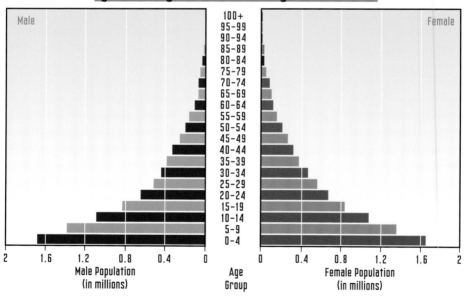

*Age distributions in nations with low birth rates take a columnar chart form (top), while age distribution charts of nations with high birth rates look more like pyramids (bottom). This reflects the fact that nations with high birth rates typically have far more young people than elderly people, while nations with lower birth rates have more evenly distributed numbers of people across age groupings.*

## World Demographics by Region in 2013

| REGION | POPULATION | BR | DR | GR (%) | LE (YEARS) |
|--------|-----------|-----|-----|--------|------------|
| World | 7,095,262,215 | 19 | 10 | 1.1 | 71 |
| Asia | 4,298,966,164 | 17 | 7 | 1.0 | 72 |
| Africa | 1,128,468,418 | 33 | 10 | 2.3 | 59 |
| Europe | 720,671,119 | 11 | 11 | 0.1 | 76 |
| North America | 551,340,932 | 15 | 7 | 0.9 | 78 |
| South America | 402,380,959 | 15 | 6 | 0.9 | 74 |

*This chart shows aggregate data on birth rates (BR), death rates (DR), growth rates (GR), and life expectancies (LE) for the world and for all major continents in 2013. The African birth rate of 33 is more than twice as large as the North American birth rate of 15. As one would expect, the African growth rate is also larger by about the same amount (2.3 percent versus 0.9 percent). Life expectancies are also dramatically different—fifty-nine years in Africa and seventy-eight years in North America.*

## EQUILIBRIUMS—AND WHY THEY MATTER

An equilibrium occurs when a society's population is neither rising nor falling in numbers. This means the number of people born into that society is matched by the numbers who are dying. A nation may have an equilibrium in which both birth rates and death rates are high. In this scenario, the average life expectancy is very low. This situation was common in ancient times and is found in the twenty-first century in very poor populations such as in Zimbabwe and Niger. On the other hand, a nation may have an equilibrium in which birth rates and death rates are both low and life expectancies are high. This is the case in Japan and in many European nations of the twenty-first century. In European countries such as Denmark and Germany, people enjoy high life expectancies and a very high quality of life. The difference in the quality of life between these two types of equilibriums is stunning.

At equilibrium, a nation's population growth is zero. Life expectancy in equilibrium populations is definable as 1,000 divided by birth rates. In the long run, birth rates, like death rates, determine life expectancy. The ability to maintain the living systems that support all human life on Earth rests on keeping birth rates low. If we cannot successfully control birth rates around the globe, we will create a world in which life expectancy will be shortened for everyone.

# CHAPTER 2
# MIGRATIONS

Remember, remember always, that all of us,

Siberia

EUROPE

ASIA

Middle
East

China

AFRICA

AUSTRALIA

The story of civilization is one long tale of migrations with big consequences. *Homo erectus* (our early human ancestors) migrated from Africa to Asia and Europe at least two hundred thousand years ago. Our own *Homo sapiens* crossed into the Western Hemisphere from Asia about thirty thousand to fifty thousand years ago.

In ancient times, especially before the development of agriculture, many people lived in groups that moved often to follow game or to move herds of livestock to new pastures. In some parts of the modern world, this nomadic culture endures among peoples such as the Bedouin and Tuareg of North Africa, for example, and among some Tibetans and Mongolians of Asia. Nomads are difficult for demographers to track because these societies move regularly and often don't report births and

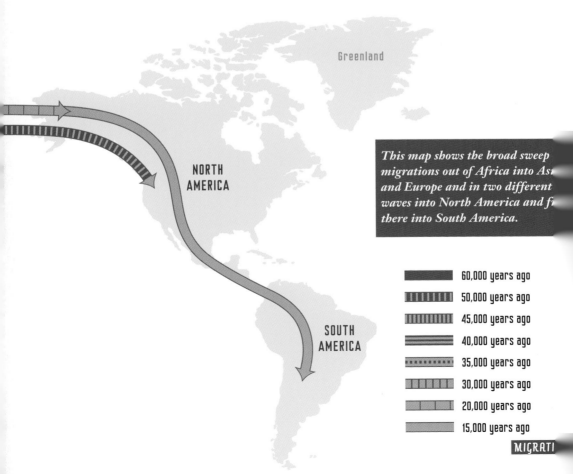

Greenland

NORTH
AMERICA

*This map shows the broad sweep*
*migrations out of Africa into As*
*and Europe and in two different*
*waves into North America and fi*
*there into South America.*

SOUTH
AMERICA

| | |
|---|---|
| | 60,000 years ago |
| | 50,000 years ago |
| | 45,000 years ago |
| | 40,000 years ago |
| | 35,000 years ago |
| | 30,000 years ago |
| | 20,000 years ago |
| | 15,000 years ago |

deaths to central authorities. For this reason, official population counts of nomadic peoples are relatively inaccurate.

As agriculture developed, populations grew—a lot. During the last ten thousand years, empires expanded, contracted, and clashed hundreds of times. Violent clashes have caused people to migrate hundreds or sometimes even thousands of miles from where they were born.

In the early twenty-first century, the big population migration flows are from Central America to North and South America, from eastern Europe into western Europe, and from Africa and southern Asia into many other parts of the world. Migrants flee the violence and persecution of war as well as the geographic upheaval of natural disasters. Mostly, migrants flee poverty. Many people are looking for better economic opportunities at all times. A global trend of the twenty-first century indicates that people are also leaving rural areas for jobs in urban settings. In general, people move along opportunity gradients,

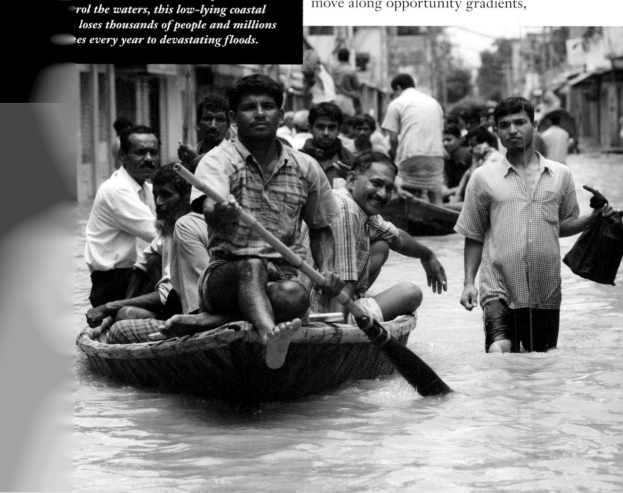

*ns migrate for many reasons, often to atural disasters. Flooding is common gladesh (below), for example, where rains hit every year during the nation's on season. With limited infrastructure rol the waters, this low-lying coastal loses thousands of people and millions es every year to devastating floods.*

from places of less opportunity (or greater danger) to places with more opportunity or less danger.

## THE FOURTH VARIABLE

Demographers consider migration one of the primary population variables. Migration, into a country or out of it and into another country, can impact a nation's growth rates significantly. For example, if one thousand people are immigrating every year into a population of one hundred thousand people, that community's growth rate will increase by 1 percent. Conversely, if that population was losing one thousand people each year to emigration, the growth rate would be reduced by 1 percent. One percent may seem insignificant, but with growth rates, it can translate into large numbers of people.

People moving into a community bring with them both positive and negative potentials. They bring talents, and they bring needs. Adults need jobs. Children need schooling, and both adults and children need health care. Needs are especially great when people are fleeing wars. Those migrants typically arrive bearing emotional scars and with little money or other resources to reestablish a new life. This translates into financial costs for the host community to meet housing, medical, and other needs of the new immigrants.

Immigrants also bring valuable skills, such as contributing to a destination country's labor force. Many immigrants are especially entrepreneurial and set up new businesses that thrive in the destination country. However, if large numbers of immigrants come into a community quickly, harsh consequences may follow.

A dramatic historical example of such consequences faced the peoples in Minnesota Territory in the 1800s. At

## The Statue of Liberty

Give me your tired, your poor,

Your huddled masses yearning to breathe free,

The wretched refuse of your teeming shore.

Send these, the homeless, tempest-tost to me,

I lift my lamp beside the golden door!

—Emma Lazarus, "New Colossus," 1883

the beginning of that century, 99 percent of the people in Minnesota were Native Americans. A few hundred French Canadians and their mixed-blood descendants lived in a colony called Pembina near what is now Minnesota's border with Canada. In 1900, just one century later, 99 percent of the people in what had become the state of Minnesota were whites of European extraction. This dramatic demographic shift occurred as more than 1.5 million white immigrants seeking land to farm moved into Minnesota, overwhelming the area's thirty thousand original Dakota Sioux and Ojibwa inhabitants. Many of the Sioux died or were driven out after a six-week war between the Dakota Sioux and the US Army in 1862 over control of the land. Through the pressures of intense migration and a subsequent war, the destiny of Minnesota's original inhabitants was forever changed.

## BRAIN DRAINS

Many countries worry about losing the skills of citizens who choose to emigrate. For example, Colombia in South America has a law restricting emigration of doctors and other skilled health professionals trained at the country's academies. This law was enacted in the 1990s because so many health-care workers were moving abroad to seek higher incomes. Not enough remained to care for Colombia's citizens. Strict rules about traveling to other countries dominated the nations of the Soviet Union (fifteen republics, including Russia) and eastern Europe under twentieth-century Communist rule. In those societies, Jews and other minority groups faced discrimination in education, jobs, and housing. They and other citizens who wanted to form their own businesses were often discouraged from doing so, leading many to escape to freer countries. Destination countries benefited from the businesses these entrepreneurial immigrants started. One famous example is Google, cofounded by Sergey Brin. His family, who is Jewish, left Russia in the 1970s, eventually moving to the United States. There, Brin went to college and met Larry Page with whom he founded the Internet company when they were graduate students at Stanford University in California. Google is now a multibillion-dollar corporation recognized around the world.

Romania provides another, more recent example from post-Communist eastern Europe. When a global recession began in 2007, better educated and more employable Romanians began seeking opportunities in richer countries of the European Union (EU) to the west. Romania lost about 2.4 million people from 2001 to the most recent census in 2012. That is roughly 12 percent of the entire population of Romania, which dropped during that time frame from 21.4 million to 19 million people. If this large outflow were to continue for one hundred years, no Romanians would be left in Romania.

Other examples of brain drains can be found across Africa, many nations of which desperately need the talents of their doctors, engineers, lawyers, and other skilled professionals. However, many skilled workers in African nations leave to find similar jobs that pay much more in Europe, Asia, and the Americas. Other nations such as Iran also suffer annual losses of well-educated young people, who flee political repression in search of more freedom.

Nobel Peace Prize–winning human rights attorney and former judge Shirin Ebadi of Iran described the situation in her 2006 book *Iran Awakening*. She commented, "The estimates are rough, but approximately four to five million Iranians left over two decades [following the Islamic Revolution of 1979], among the country's brightest. To this day, Iran sustains one of the most serious brain drains in the world. Those of us who stayed have watched our young people fan out across the world, animating the societies and economies of nations other than our own."

> To this day, Iran sustains one of the most serious brain drains in the world. Those of us who stayed have watched our young people fan out across the world, animating the societies and economies of nations other than our own.
>
> —*Shirin Ebadi*, Iran Awakening, *2006*

## LEGAL AND ILLEGAL MIGRATIONS

Most countries in the twenty-first century world have laws controlling the numbers of immigrants they will accept each year. Some nations have laws regulating emigration too. In a crowded world, most countries make it easier for a person to leave than to enter on a permanent basis, unless that person has rare and desirable job skills. Most countries have special provisions for entry of people from skilled professions. In the United States, for example, the H1-B Visa makes it easier for people with critical job skills to enter the country and find work with a US company.

Immigration laws in the United States create two broad categories of immigrants: those who have gone through public processes and have documents allowing them to be legal resident noncitizens in the United States, and those who did not go through legal processes. Without required legal documentation, immigrants to the United States can be deported to their country of origin. The total number of legal, resident noncitizens in the United States in 2011 was about 13.1 million people, of whom about 30 percent were originally from Mexico. The US government also estimated that about 12 million people without legal papers were living in the United States that year. In a total US population of just over 300 million people in 2011, 25 million residents who are not citizens is a significant part of the population (8 percent).

The legal status of immigrants can have profound effects on every aspect of life, both for them and for the country

*rt controls at airports around the check traveler documentation to that people are entering a country . Here, travelers holding European rts pass through a checkpoint at an t in the United Kingdom.*

they live in. Legal status often determines whether a person is an asset for the society he or she lives in or a burden. Without proper legal documentation, immigrants are generally unable to find permanent, high-paying jobs. The jobs they do find—such as washing dishes in restaurants or working in meatpacking plants—may contribute to society, but they are often low paying and not permanent. On the other hand, immigrants with all the required legal documentation typically find it easier to get jobs, to pursue higher education, and to put down roots in their communities. In general, stable communities place less strain on societies, and in this way, legal immigrants are much easier for a society to absorb.

# CHAPTER 3
# ASIA

In China, the rich can pay a fine and have a second child.

—New York Times, *website introduction to Ma*
*"China's Brutal One-Child Policy," Opinion Pages, May 22*

More than half of the people on Earth (about 60 percent) live in Asia. The Asian continent includes fifty-one countries, two of which (Russia and Turkey) straddle both the Asian and the European continents. For this reason, significant portions of the Russian and Turkish populations are actually in Europe. The biggest Asian nations by population—China and India—have growing populations with more than one billion people each and are among the most dynamic economies of the world. But they also have some of the deepest poverty in the world, especially in rural areas. This poverty contributes to high death rates and lower life expectancy. Japan is the only country in Asia whose population is shrinking. This is due to very low birth rates and to a very successful high-tech economy that yields the highest life expectancy in the twenty-first century world.

*...tion pressures in China ...tense. For example, ...hai is one of China's ...t cities, with a population ...e than 20 million people. ... of this, the city has a ...floating population of ...two million workers.*

## Demographics of the Largest Countries in Asia in 2013

| COUNTRY | POPULATION (MILLIONS) | BR | DR | GR (%) | LE (YEARS) |
|---|---|---|---|---|---|
| China | 1,350 | 12.3 | 7.3 | 0.46 | 75.0 |
| India | 1,221 | 20.2 | 7.4 | 1.28 | 67.5 |
| Indonesia | 251 | 17.4 | 6.3 | 0.99 | 71.9 |
| Pakistan | 193 | 23.8 | 6.7 | 1.52 | 66.7 |
| Bangladesh | 164 | 22.1 | 5.7 | 1.59 | 70.4 |
| Japan | 127 | 8.2 | 9.3 | –0.10 | 84.2 |

*While China had about 129 million more people than India in 2013, India's growth rate is much larger than China's. If that trend continues, India's population will surpass China's somewhere between 2025 and 2030.*

Population pressures vary dramatically around the world. For example, the well-developed, high-tech, and stable economy of Japan can support far more people comfortably than can less developed, lower-tech economies such as those of Myanmar and Vietnam. This is true even though Japan, with rocky terrain and limited farmland, must import much of its food. By contrast, Myanmar and Vietnam both have more arable land and rely less on food imports. Nonetheless, with a healthier economy overall, Japan is better able to support large numbers of people by trade with other nations.

## CHINA

China has the largest population and one of the highest life expectancies in Asia. It also has the second-lowest birth rate after Japan. This wasn't always the case. By the mid-twentieth century, Chinese demographers had recognized that the nation's large population and high birth rates were leading to devastating famines with every bad harvest. During China's famines, millions of people starved to death and the nation was unable to compete with other global economies. Eager to grow stronger in a world where other countries were leaping forward economically, China listened to its demographers. Chinese government leaders decided that given demographic realities, the only way to compete globally was to reduce the constant population pressure that was linked to high birth rates, high death rates, and unsolvable poverty.

To achieve this goal, China put the one-child policy into place in 1979, mandating only one child for most families. This policy—in a culture that reveres children, large families, and ancestral heritage—was a huge shock to many Chinese people. To enforce the one-child laws, every village has a minor governmental official, almost always a woman, whose job is to keep track of the other women's families and fertility. If a woman conceives more than one child during her years of fertility, she is often forced to have an abortion or is sterilized. And because Chinese culture values boys over girls, many female fetuses are aborted by the parent's choice. As a result, far more boy babies are born in China than girl babies. In the twenty-first century, about 120 boy babies are recorded in China for every 100 girl babies.

# One-Child Exceptions

The Chinese government has allowed for some exceptions to the nation's one-child policy. For example, a member of an ethnic minority or a rural farmer who needs a larger family to help run the farm may apply for and get permission from local officials to have an additional child if the firstborn is female. Other exemptions include couples in which each partner is a single child or in cases where the firstborn are twins.

China enforces its one-child policy through income-based fines on families who violate the policy. The enforcement is not consistent, however. Violations among government officials, for example, are routinely ignored. In addition, people may pay bribes to local officials to allow their family to have more than one child. Rich people may simply pay the fines that poor Chinese cannot afford.

为四化一对夫妇只生一个孩

*A Chinese poster glorifies the nation's one-child policy, which has been law since the late 1970s. In practice, many people circumvent the policy by paying bribes, while in other cases, women abort unwanted girl fetuses.*

American journalist Eleanor Clift wrote a long, investigative essay on gender imbalances in Asia in a 2011 article titled "Asia's 163 Million Missing Girls." In it, she notes that "China's one-child policy was put in place . . . before ultrasound technology was widely available and used to determine the sex of a fetus. Three decades later, an imbalance of boys over girls that has been made possible by gender selection abortion practices is visible not only in China, but in India and other developing countries—and in ethnic Asian communities in the United States."

Tens of millions of abortions were performed in the early years of the one-child policy and within a generation, China was dominated by single child families. The policy, which continues into the twenty-first century, led to the reduction of out-of-control population growth and crippling famine and created a stable population to provide the labor force necessary to compete economically on a global scale. As a program of social control, it is highly controversial, is unpopular in China, and has not been adopted in any other part of the world.

## JAPAN

Japan is the most developed economy in Asia, with advanced, modern technologies and practices. Japan's birth rate is also by far the lowest in Asia, and the life expectancy of Japanese people, at 84.2 years, is greater than that of any other Asian country. High levels of education and a strong economy encourage both low birth rates and high life expectancies.

Why are Japan's birth rate and growth rate so much lower than China's even though Japan does not have a one-child policy? In Japan birth rates have been suppressed not by policy but by thousands of individual decisions to limit the size of families. After Japan's devastating loss in World War II (1939–1945), citizens and the government promoted population control through contraception and abstinence. They recognized the limits of Japan's natural resources to support large numbers of people and therefore worked to ensure sustainable population numbers. Japan quickly achieved the columnar age distribution associated with developed countries.

In the twenty-first century, Japan faces unexpected consequences of its success in controlling population: Birth rates are lower than death

# The Koreas

For thousands of years, the Korean people were one culture occupying a tiny peninsula attached to China. After World War II, Korea became two separate nations—a Communist North Korea, sponsored by the Soviet Union and China, and a capitalist South Korea, sponsored by the United States. The Korean War (1950–1953) between these alliances killed millions of people. Starvation was common, and refugee populations—in desperate need of fuel—cut down almost all of Korea's woodlands.

The two nations did not recover in equal measure from that war. In the twenty-first century, North Korea is largely cut off from the rest of the world. It has about 24 million people, most of whom are desperately poor. The state-controlled economy is weak, population growth rates are moderate at 0.54 percent per year, and life expectancy is only about sixty-nine years. In contrast, South Korea has very successfully rebounded. Its population is twice as big (about 50 million people), life expectancy is at least ten years greater (seventy-nine-plus years), and the economy is about forty times larger than North Korea's.

rates. And the average age in Japan—44.6 years—is older than in any other major country. These two factors have led to a negative growth rate, and Japan's population is beginning to shrink. As a result, Japan has fewer young people in the workplace to help provide pensions to elders, who are living much longer than their ancestors did.

## INDONESIA AND BANGLADESH

Indonesia is the world's largest Muslim country, and its growth rates rank in the middle of those of the six largest countries in Asia. Indonesia is unique in that its population is scattered among more than three thousand islands. Conflicts with neighbors are therefore rare, and limits on expansion are clear. Indonesia tries to find a middle way to develop its economy faster than its population grows. It also practices moderate forms of Islam, which encourage greater autonomy for women, allowing them to control their fertility, education, and life planning, and thereby leading to lower birth rates.

With 164 million people in 2013, Bangladesh is the eighth-largest country in the world by population, but it is not a large country in area. Half of the nation is a huge river delta that floods during almost every rainy season. Bangladesh is also one of the poorest countries in the world. The annual flooding leads to mass migrations as the large number of poor people living in the floodplains flee the rising waters.

Why are so many people living on floodplains? In a crowded country such as Bangladesh, land is very limited. People crowd into whatever space is available, including the floodplains. In addition, when the delta is dry, it is extremely fertile, so farmers settle there to grow food crops. However, the floods return almost every rainy season. As global warming intensifies, sea levels are rising. Because Bangladesh is a coastal nation, this may create even more population dislocation.

## PAKISTAN

Pakistan has the highest birth rate of the six largest nations in Asia. It also has the second-highest growth rate and among the lowest life expectancies, partly because of a high rate of violence. Pakistan has very limited natural resources, yet its population grows by about 4 million people every year.

Pakistan's population has increased from 34 million in 1951 to 193 million in 2013. That is a 568 percent increase in sixty-two years. For decades, Pakistan had no population policy at all. In 2010 the government adopted a new population policy, promising to boost support for family planning services. But such measures take a generation or more to have their full effect and they face resistance from traditionalists, who seldom support family planning measures.

One of the ways people may respond to population pressure is to fight over resources. This is true in Pakistan, where daily violence characterizes the struggle over political and economic power. There is also a long-running dispute between Pakistan and India over the border territory of Kashmir, which is rich in water, timber, and farmable land. With intense population pressures, Pakistan would like to tap into those resources.

## Oceania

Australia and New Zealand are the largest countries in what some geographers call Oceania or Australasia. This region includes many small island nations of the Pacific Ocean. Together, Australia and New Zealand have almost 27 million people, with birth rates in the low teens, death rates about seven per thousand, and growth rates averaging 1 percent. These demographics are similar to those of the Americas.

*Poverty and violence are among the many factors that lead to low life expectancy in Pakistan. The nation's largest city, Karachi, is home to more than 23 million people, almost half of whom live in urban squalor like this young girl.*

*s growing middle class* (above)—*a result
economic boom in manufacturing, foreign
ment, and outsourcing services—began to
e pinch as the global economic downturn
d inflation and declining retail sales
2013. India has Asia's third-largest
ny yet the second-lowest life expectancy of
ntinent's six largest nations.*

## INDIA

After China, India is the other
giant among world nations, with
more than 1.2 billion people
and a population that is growing
by about 17 million each year.
Because of extreme poverty, poor education, polluted water, and lack of
health care among millions of its citizens, India has the second-lowest
life expectancy of the six biggest Asian nations. Yet its economic growth
rate is substantial. While about 800 million Indians remain in abject
rural poverty, the other 400 million are leaping into a global middle
class, and some are quite rich. In 2012 General Shankar Roychowdhury,
a retired chief of staff of the Indian Army, observed that if India had
been able to keep its population at 1965 levels (about 500 million people),
it would be one of the twenty-first century's most developed nations.
To Roychowdhury, population growth is a bigger security threat to
India than is China, its political adversary to the north, or Pakistan, its
neighbor to the west with which it has fought three wars since 1947.

India's rising population creates intense pressures on its citizens,
and it also impacts wildlife populations. As the nation cuts down forests
to create more land for growing food crops, wild animals lose precious
habitat. For example, India's wild tiger population is almost extinct. The
same is true for wild Indian elephants and hundreds of other creatures

and plants in the nation's dwindling rain forests. This is not just a loss for Asia but for the whole world and for the children of our future. Since human existence is dependent upon the success of the rest of the living systems on Earth, the prospect of so many extinctions is alarming to many scientists around the world.

With its large human population, India also faces intense pressure to find new water resources. The massive Himalayan mountains form the border between India and China. They are the highest mountains in the world and capture huge amounts of snow during rainy monsoon seasons. They are also the site of mighty glaciers, which are a key source of water for irrigating croplands that support about two billion people in India, China, and several smaller countries in the region. Facing the prospect of vanishing glaciers as a result of global warming—and with no other obvious source of water to replace them—scientists and farmers are racing to find ways to better conserve water and to grow larger volumes of food as available waters decline.

# Global Warming

Global warming is caused mainly by increasing levels of carbon dioxide in the air from burning fossil fuels such as oil, coal, natural gas, and other carbon sources, such as forests. Most of the new carbon dioxide in the atmosphere comes from motor vehicles and coal-powered electricity plants. Atmospheric carbon dioxide was at record levels in the year 2014, and efforts to reduce production of carbon dioxide have been difficult to achieve for political and economic reasons. The United States and developing nations such as China and India top the list of nations that pump the most carbon dioxide into the atmosphere.

Most scientists agree that global warming is leading to rising sea levels, an intensification of violent storms, and melting glaciers and polar ice caps. It is also behind the increased acidification of the oceans, which is killing coral reefs around the world. These situations can be devastating, particularly when they impact high-population areas with limited economic resources.

# CHAPTER 4
# EUROPE

The number of people on our earth, and the rate

at which we are consuming the earth's resources, underlies all other concerns about conservation, food security, women's empowerment, protection of wildlife and all species, security of nations, equality among peoples and the purity of the very air, water and soil on which we all survive.

—*Marianne Gabel, attorney and member of Population Connection Board of Directors, 2013*

*In need of workers, the Russian region of Siberia has turned to Chinese immigrant labor, who are willing to share tight quarters (left) and to accept relatively low wages. The ethnic demographics of Europe continue to shift as economic forces drive ethnically diverse peoples from other parts of the world to look for jobs there.*

The United Nations counts about 721 million people in the countries of Europe in 2013, or 10 percent of the world's population. Five of those countries, including Russia and Turkey, straddle the European and Asian continents. Demographers sometimes view Russians living east of the Ural Mountains and Turks living east of the Bosporus Strait as Asians. This lowers the population figure for Europe to about 615 million people, or 9 percent of the world's population.

Italy, France, and the United Kingdom have growth rates of about 0.5 percent per year, falling roughly in the middle of overall European growth rates. Each of these three nations has slightly more than 60 million people, who enjoy high life expectancies (eighty

# Siberia

Russia's population is in decline. This trend is having big demographic consequences in Siberia, a region of harshly cold weather in Russia's Far East. Siberia has always been thinly populated, and historically, many Siberian towns and companies depended on subsidies from the Russian government to survive. In 1991, when the Soviet Union split up, Russia could no longer afford to support Siberia economically to the same degree it once had. As a result, many Siberian factories and schools closed. Large numbers of newly unemployed Siberians left the region to find better economic options elsewhere. Filling the void that persists in twenty-first century Siberia are peoples from neighboring China and Mongolia. They are willing to work hard at a lower standard of living than ethnic Russians. If this trend continues, Siberia will eventually have a largely Asian population and will no longer be ethnically Siberian.

to eighty-two years). Birth rates have been dropping dramatically in Europe since the 1960s, however, when the first effective and safe hormonally based birth control pills were invented. For this reason, Europe may be the first continent to see a decline in overall human population sometime during the next century. This shift from relatively high birth rates and near constant population growth to low birth rates and low growth has been called a demographic transition. Such transitions can have financial and physical consequences as significant as the exploding populations of very poor countries.

## Demographics of the Largest Countries in Europe in 2013

| COUNTRY | POPULATION (MILLIONS) | BR | DR | GR (%) | LE (YEARS) |
|---|---|---|---|---|---|
| Russia[1] | 110.0 | 12.1 | 14.0 | −0.02 | 69.8 |
| Germany | 81.2 | 8.4 | 11.2 | −0.19 | 80.3 |
| France | 66.0 | 12.6 | 9.0 | 0.47 | 81.6 |
| United Kingdom | 63.4 | 12.3 | 9.3 | 0.55 | 80.3 |
| Italy | 61.5 | 8.9 | 10.0 | 0.34 | 82.0 |
| Turkey[2] | 11.7 | 17.2 | 6.1 | 1.16 | 73.0 |

[1] *Total population of 142.5, with 32.5 million in Asia*

[2] *Total population of 80.7 million, with 69 million in Asia*

*A generalized migration is in progress from the poorer countries of the European Union and near neighbors such as Belarus into the richer countries of the EU in the west and north. In the table above, the significantly lower life expectancies of Russia and Turkey stand out against higher life expectancies of Germany and other northern and western nations of the EU.*

# TRADEOFFS

The low birth rates in Europe result in population growth rates that are very near zero (0.1 percent for Europe in 2013, compared with the much higher rates of 1.0 percent in Asia, 0.9 percent in North America, 0.9 percent in South America, and 2.3 percent in Africa). Assuming a nation has sufficient natural and economic resources, it can usually support its population if overall birth rates are low. This balance of population to resources leads to high standards of living. In fact, western Europeans have the twenty-first century's highest average standard of living among continents on Earth. Low birth rates in western Europe also result in a higher ratio of older people to younger people. This age distribution puts economic pressures on European societies, whose elders typically require more health care, payouts of pensions, and other economic social supports.

People living on the poorer continents of Africa and Asia are often eager to fill job opportunities in the richer countries of Europe. But large numbers of immigrants to Europe, especially those who do not share European cultural traditions such as language, religion, and culinary habits, can place social and political strains on host nations. In many instances, host communities are not willing or able to quickly adapt to the changing racial and cultural demographics they face. Racial and religious tensions sometimes break out in violence, especially in nations that were once racially homogenous.

## DEMOGRAPHIC TRANSITIONS AND BIRTH CONTROL

Demographic transitions such as the shift to low growth rates in Europe are usually associated with higher levels of education and economic development. Access to education, jobs, and social safety nets (such as the Social Security program in the United States) helps reduce birth rates and is almost always correlated with lower birth rates. But the most powerful factor of all appears to be the degree to which women are freed from tribal practices and customs that prioritize motherhood as a mission (or even a duty) and that often legally restrict women's freedoms.

The most directly related of these factors is women's control, or lack thereof, of reproductive behavior and medical care.

Birth rates typically fall when women have access to affordable, effective birth control methods and to safe and legal abortion. This has occurred in European nations such as Denmark, France, and

*Families in western Europe have easy access to birth control, family planning services, and medical care. The standard of living in this part of the world is the globe's highest.*

Germany, where birth control is easily accessible—and free. This link between birth control technologies (such as the pill and condoms, among various options) and lowering birth rates also affects the UN's global development programs, which usually include access to birth control as an essential part of women's health care.

Demographers also see a direct correlation between developing economies, access to birth control, and dropping birth rates. For example, as European and North American economies boomed in the 1960s and as birth control pills became widely available, demographers observed dramatic drops in birth rates. They hoped that economic development alone might also reduce high birth rates in poor nations as those countries gained wealth and offered better medical care and education to more citizens. To a degree, this has occurred, especially when societies can create social safety nets to free elders from dependence on their descendants. All the same, declines in birth rates typically take decades to fully impact a nation's overall demographic profile, and they are never automatic, responding to both traditional and popular culture.

## CULTURAL CROSSROADS

Turkey has been a crossroads between Europe and Asia for thousands of years, both geographically and culturally. As part of a decades-long effort to modernize along Western models, Turkey has worked exceptionally hard to emancipate women from ancient social constraints, to promote secular (nonreligious) government over theocracy (a government in which a god is recognized as the ruler), and to replace its Arabic-style alphabet with a Latin alphabet. Demographically, the most significant aspects of Turkey for many Europeans are its birth rates and growth rates. Although lower than many more strictly Islamic nations, these rates are much higher than European rates.

Some Europeans fear that Turkish immigrants could overwhelm original peoples in northern European countries. For example, when looking at age distributions for Germany and Turkey, demographers see a classical columnar age distribution for Germany (with a higher average age) and a pyramid-shaped age distribution for Turkey (with more young in each layer than elders). Turkey is actually in the early

Turkey straddles the European and [Asi]an continents and is a society in [wh]ich European and traditional Islamic [val]ues intermingle. This is evident on [the] streets of large Turkish cities, such [as I]stanbul (above), whose population [of m]ore than 10 million people accept [cul]tural differences with relative ease.

stages of demographic transition. Its birth rates are dropping, and in the long run, it will probably achieve a columnar age distribution and stable population size. But the average age of Turks is still a young twenty-eight years. Because of the momentum of growth associated with pyramidal age distributions, Turkey could be twice as large as it is today when its population finally stabilizes.

Turkey lies close to European nations such as Germany and Italy, which have stable or declining populations. For decades Turkish immigrants have been a prime source of labor for these and other nations of the European Union, a political and economic association of twenty-seven member nations. Turkey has applied for membership in the EU but has not yet been accepted, partly due to its relatively high birth rates compared with current members. Long ago, Germany made special laws to allow for guest workers from Turkey to come to Germany to live and work. By the twenty-first century, Germany was home to at least five million Turks. The children of Turkish

*German politicians of Turkish descent* (above) *attend a political convention in Hannover, Germany. Many of the children of Turkish guest workers who arrived in the 1960s have become fully integrated into German society. On the other hand, they and more recent immigrants still face racial and ethnic discrimination in Germany.*

guest workers, born and schooled in Germany, think of themselves in all ways German, and they are legally full citizens. However, many Turks still face discrimination and racial hatred from some sectors of German society because of differences in religion (many Turks practice Islam) and other cultural traditions. With higher birth rates, ethnic Turks may actually outnumber ethnic Germans in Germany by the year 2050.

In order to stabilize human population growth,

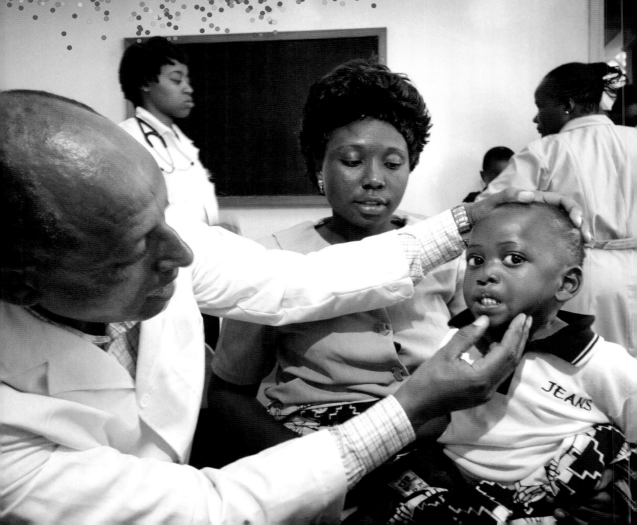

Africa has more than one billion people, about 15 percent of the world's entire population. In fact, 76 percent of the world's people live in either Africa or Asia. Europe has about 10 percent of the world's total population; South America, 9 percent; and North America, 5 percent. In 2013 Africa's population was increasing by about 23 million people per year. This makes Africa the second most populated continent on Earth (after Asia), and the fastest growing.

The range of economic conditions in Africa is vast, from the desperately poor Democratic Republic of Congo and Zimbabwe to relatively well-developed Egypt and South Africa. Africa's GR is more than twice that of any other continent at 2.3 percent per year, dwarfing Europe's 0.1 percent overall population growth rate. The 2.3 percent growth rate per year in Africa implies a doubling time of thirty years if that rate is sustained (70/2.3 = 30).

Africa has many natural, though limited, resources, which cannot double in thirty years to keep pace with population growth. One important demographic consequence of this imbalance of people to resources is migration out of Africa into Europe, Asia, and the Americas. That often includes better educated, skilled, or wealthy Africans, creating a serious brain drain across the African continent.

*An Ethiopian doctor working for an international health organization treats a young child in Tanzania. With limited resources, burgeoning populations, and deep poverty, the African continent has lost doctors and many other skilled professionals to more lucrative opportunities in other parts of the world.*

# Losing Gorillas and Chimpanzees

As the human population in Africa grows, so does construction, agriculture, timber harvesting, and other development projects. One of the most significant consequences of this development is the destruction of the last wild habitats on Earth for animals such as chimpanzees and gorillas. The Great Lakes Region of central Africa is home to the world's few remaining chimpanzees (one hundred thousand to two hundred thousand) and gorillas. Only about 620 mountain gorillas remained in the wild in 2013. About 100,000 eastern and western lowland gorillas may still exist in the jungles of four Central African countries.

The Great Lakes Region includes Rwanda, Burundi, Tanzania, and other countries around Lake Victoria and Lake Tanganyika. The mountains in Rwanda are among the last habitats on Earth for mountain gorillas. Many of the globe's remaining chimpanzees live in the jungles of eastern Congo, where decades of violence between militias and warlords have killed millions of people. As desperate Congolese flee the murderous militias, they often survive by eating bushmeat, a term for the meat of wildlife. This meat often includes that of chimpanzees.

Jane Goodall, a world-famous anthropologist and primatologist, has spent most of her adult life studying chimpanzees in the Gombe Stream National Park of Tanzania on the east bank of Lake Tanganyika. Her work has focused on researching primate behavior and advocating for the protection of chimpanzees and the environment. Through her Jane Goodall Institute, which she founded in the 1970s, she is recognized as a global leader in working to protect chimpanzees and their habitats through conservation programs in Africa and other parts of the world. Her Roots and Shoots program helps young people around the world design, lead, and put into practice their own projects for making the world a better place for humans and animals.

Another consequence is the failure of national governments, as has occurred in Somalia, Mali, and eastern Congo. In those African nations, population growth has severely outstripped national resources. The ensuing struggle over control of resources, among other issues, has led to destabilized governments and long-term civil conflicts.

Africa is a tremendously diverse continent, with fifty-two nations and hundreds of languages. In Nigeria alone, more than four hundred languages and distinct dialects are spoken. Nigeria is the largest country in Africa, and almost every African country includes peoples from different language groups, tribes, and cultures. Morocco on the northwestern coast has nine different official languages. South Africa recognizes eleven distinct tribes, nine black and two white. The latter speak either English or Afrikaans (derived from Dutch).

*With almost 3 million people, Kano is the largest city in Nigeria. In the two decades from 1990 to 2008, Nigeria experienced a 60 percent population growth rate. Nigeria is Africa's most populated nation and makes up almost 20 percent of the continent's human citizens.*

The former speak IsiXhosa, IsiZulu, Sesotho sa Leboa, Sesotho, Setswana, siSwati, Tshivenda, or Xitsonga, with many distinct dialects within these core language groups. This extreme cultural complexity combines with high population pressure, relatively young governments, and arbitrary national borders (a vestige of colonial times) that ignore historical ethnic boundaries to create a large number of ethnic tensions.

| Demographics of the Six Biggest Countries in Africa (by population) in 2013 | | | | | |
|---|---|---|---|---|---|
| COUNTRY | POPULATION | BR | DR | GR (%) | LE (YEARS) |
| Nigeria | 174,508,000 | 38.8 | 13.2 | 2.54 | 52.5 |
| Ethiopia | 93,877,000 | 38.1 | 8.9 | 2.90 | 60.0 |
| Egypt | 85,294,000 | 23.8 | 4.8 | 1.88 | 73.2 |
| Dem. Rep. Congo | 75,507,000 | 36.3 | 10.5 | 2.54 | 56.1 |
| South Africa | 48,601,000 | 19.1 | 17.4 | –0.45 | 49.5 |
| Tanzania | 48,261,000 | 37.3 | 8.4 | 2.82 | 60.8 |

*With the exception of South Africa, which is besieged by an HIV/AIDS epidemic, the continent of Africa has by far the highest birth rates and population growth rates in the world. These correlate with low life expectancies and limited social safety nets.*

# BURSTING AT THE SEAMS—AND LOW LIFE EXPECTANCIES

While the populations of most African nations are growing rapidly, the more developed economies within Africa, such as Egypt and South Africa, have birth rates of 24 and 19, respectively. These are high compared to the rest of the world but low for Africa. Egypt also has by far the lowest death rate among the six largest African nations. South Africa has the highest death rate at 17.4, with a corresponding contrast in the population growth rates of these two countries.

South Africa is another country whose population is actually shrinking in the twenty-first century. The main reason for the shrinking population there is the HIV/AIDS epidemic, which has killed millions of Africans in the young and middle-age ranges. This contributes to South Africa's very low life expectancy at birth of forty-nine years. While HIV/AIDS is a global health problem, it is far more severe in Africa, where public health resources are limited and sociocultural attitudes toward discussing and practicing safe sex are very restrictive.

## PRESSURES ON THE YOUNG

As in other parts of the developing world, millions of people in Africa are moving from rural areas into cities all over the continent. They are seeking opportunity, like most migrants everywhere. Yet the cities do not have enough jobs to support the influx of people.

More than half of Africa's urban immigrants are under the age of twenty-five. This is typical of fast-growing populations that have many more young people than old. Young people have energy, enthusiasm, and creativity. They bring these strengths to the labor force, if and where jobs are available. And if banks will lend them start-up funds, they can start their own businesses.

But populations with many young people can also be unstable. This is especially true if large numbers of a community's young people are poorly

*Like many nations of Africa, Egypt has a very young population* (below). *About one-third of Egypt's population is fourteen years of age or younger. The number of females is about the same as that of males, unlike other nations of the world such as China, where males outnumber females.*

educated, unemployed, teenage, and male, with few productive outlets for their energy and talents. Across the world, the demographic of young, male populations in areas where jobs are scarce is the best predictor of violence, both in terms of small-scale crime and large-scale revolutions and ethnic wars. In African countries such as Mali and Somalia, young men and boys are often lured into armies to fight in ongoing conflicts that tear apart what is left of already failing countries.

The prevalence of HIV/AIDS in many parts of Africa adds to the graveness of this situation. The disease typically affects young adults just entering the most productive periods of their lives. Many of the infected young adults have very young children. When the parents die, they leave behind orphans, some of whom have HIV/AIDS themselves. With weak health-care systems across Africa and limited resources to care for orphans, the continent is faced with millions of parentless children with little stake in their communities or hope for the future.

## DESERTIFICATION

Another big problem facing Africa is desertification, in which previously productive land becomes desert. In the last few decades, for example, the southern edge of Africa's vast Sahara has crept many miles farther south as a result of this trend. Usually, long-term drought is associated with desertification. At the same time, however, relentless increases in human populations drive farmers to cut down forested areas for land to grow crops. Growth in human populations and cities also reduces the amount of land on which herdsmen can graze their livestock. In turn, herdsmen drive their livestock onto small plots of grass, where the animals eat the grasses and small bushes down to the dry ground. In both cases,

we are faced with a
[cha]nge that calls for a shift
[in] thinking, so that humanity
[stops] threatening its life-
[suppor]t system. We are called
[to ass]ist the Earth to heal her
[wound]s and in the process heal
[our ow]n—indeed to embrace
[the wh]ole of creation in all its
[divers]ity, beauty and wonder.
[Recogn]izing that sustainable
[develo]pment, democracy and
[peace] are indivisible is an idea
[whose] time has come.

—*Wangari Maathai, n.d.*

*The founder of the environmental Green Belt Movement, Wangari Maathai* (pictured here in 2002), *holds a young tree seedling. Maathai died in 2011, but the movement she created continues to tackle desertification and to provide economic opportunity to women in Kenya.*

the land is left without trees to hold soil in place, and without soil, the land becomes desert, with limited capacity to capture or retain precious rainwater.

Lack of money to address problems such as desertification has been a major stumbling block in Africa. In Kenya, however, a biologist named Wangari Maathai figured out a way to address the problem in her country. In the 1970s, she created a program to pay rural women in Kenya to plant trees and to water them during the first few critical years of tree life. Over time, her Green Belt Movement enabled thousands of Kenyan women to plant and grow more than 30 million trees. Besides providing lumber for construction and wood for cooking and heating, the trees stabilized land, held water in the soil, and provided habitat for birds and other small game. For her creative efforts in a context of deep poverty and limited education, Maathai was awarded a Nobel Peace Prize in 2004.

# CHAPTER 6
# THE
# AMERICAS

*The United States attracts immigrants from all over the world. They are following what demographers call opportunity gradients in search of a better life that offers jobs, education, health care, and freedom from violent conflict.*

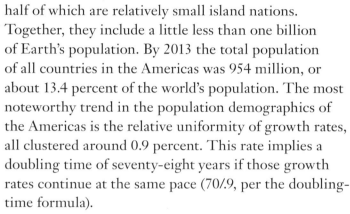

The Americas include North, Central, and South America and islands in the Caribbean Sea. That is fifty-one countries total, more than half of which are relatively small island nations. Together, they include a little less than one billion of Earth's population. By 2013 the total population of all countries in the Americas was 954 million, or about 13.4 percent of the world's population. The most noteworthy trend in the population demographics of the Americas is the relative uniformity of growth rates, all clustered around 0.9 percent. This rate implies a doubling time of seventy-eight years if those growth rates continue at the same pace (70/.9, per the doubling-time formula).

About five hundred years ago, when Christopher Columbus first landed in the Americas, the region was home to several million Native Americans. Columbus's 1492 landing triggered a long and complex history of European immigration. On the heels of European movement to the Americas came slavery and indentured servitude, bringing millions of Africans and Asians to the Western Hemisphere. This is one of the largest migrations in the history of Earth.

Large-scale population flows continue within and to the Americas, from Europe, Asia, and Africa and from Mexico and Central and South America to the United States and Canada. As in the world generally, these population flows tend to follow opportunity gradients, no matter in what direction. For example, relatively poor Central Americans are emigrating both north and south to nations with better opportunities.

El Salvador's population (6.1 million in 2013) is larger than Minnesota's (5.3 million) and is living on a land area ten times smaller. El Salvador is also mostly mountainous, so farming is difficult. Mexico's population is increasing by about 1.4 million people each year, and that nation does not have enough jobs for its citizens. For these reasons, Salvadorans, Mexicans, and other Latin Americans who face similar challenges are moving to areas within the Americas that offer more opportunities for jobs, food, and a better life overall.

Some countries such as Brazil are seeing significant internal migration. Most countries, including Brazil, have seen significant migration from rural areas into cities. But in Brazil, millions of people are also moving into the Amazon region, a vast resource-rich rain forest drained by the largest river on Earth, the Amazon. These people and the companies they work for are in quest of valuable resources such as timber, gold, oil, and land that can be ranched or farmed. To exploit these resources means cutting down rain forest land and displacing rain forest peoples.

## Demographics of the Six Largest Countries in the Americas in 2013

| COUNTRY | POPULATION | BR | DR | GR (%) | LE (YEARS) | NET MIGRATION (PER THOUSAND) |
|---|---|---|---|---|---|---|
| United States | 316,669,000 | 13.7 | 8.4 | 0.90 | 78.6 | 3.64 |
| Brazil | 201,010,000 | 15.0 | 6.5 | 0.83 | 73.0 | −0.17 |
| Mexico | 116,221,000 | 18.6 | 4.9 | 1.07 | 76.9 | −2.99 |
| Colombia | 45,746,000 | 17.2 | 5.3 | 1.10 | 75.0 | −0.66 |
| Argentina | 42,611,000 | 17.1 | 7.4 | 0.98 | 77.3 | 0.00 |
| Canada | 34,568,000 | 10.3 | 8.2 | 0.77 | 81.6 | 5.65 |

*Net international migration rates are shown on the right of this table, expressed as immigrants per thousand residents in 2013. Canada welcomed the largest number, with 5.65 immigrants per thousand resident Canadians in 2013. The negative number for Mexico (–2.99) suggests migration out of Mexico in early 2013, but improvements in Mexico's economy have ended previous large flows of migrants northward. Demographic data from governments often lags reality by one or several years. The United States and Canada attract immigrants from all over the world, of course, not just from Central America. Immigration increases population growth rates in the destination countries and reduces population growth rates in countries of origin.*

Brazil's population is very diverse, with more than one-third of all Brazilians identifying a mixed-race heritage.

# BRAZIL

Brazil is the largest country in South America, in both area and population, with 200 million people scattered over an area only slightly smaller than the entire United States. Colonized by the Portuguese, Brazil's official national language is Portuguese, unlike the rest of the continent, where Spanish prevails. Brazil's ethnic makeup is extremely diverse, with 53.7 percent white of various origins; 6.2 percent black; 38.5 percent mulatto (mixed); and 1.6 percent Japanese, Arab, indigenous, or other.

More than 81 percent of Brazilians live in cities, where great wealth exists side by side with great slums called favelas. As increasing numbers of Brazilian women receive education and enter the workforce, they are gaining more control over their reproductive health. Accordingly, birth rates and fertility rates are falling as Brazilian women choose to have smaller families. In 2012, for example, the typical Brazilian woman had fewer than two children compared to six children per woman fifty years ago.

How has Brazil achieved a lower fertility rate (1.9 children per woman) than that of the United States? The birth control pill was first introduced into Brazil in the early 1960s, and although the Catholic

Church—Brazil's main religious institution—adamantly opposes the pill, it is widely used. The Brazilian government makes contraception available through a variety of free and subsidized programs. For example, birth control pills are free at government-run pharmacies. For poor Brazilians who do not use those pharmacies, the pill is available through a government-subsidized program that greatly reduces the cost of this form of contraception. The government also distributes millions of free condoms each year as part of its anti-HIV/AIDS program, many of them before the nation's yearly Carnival (pre-Easter) celebration, known for its wild all-night parties. Vasectomies for men are also available for free at state-funded hospitals. Health kiosks at truck stops, mostly in southern Brazil, offer HIV/AIDS and other health information to truckers along with free condoms.

In addition, the nation's television viewers have been greatly impacted by television soap operas (telenovelas) in which families are portrayed as small (few if any children), urbanized, and glamorous. And as Brazil sees a real and continued migration from rural areas into the nation's cities, the telenovela scenario has become reality. While agriculturally based families need many children to help with farm labor, city life, with its heavier financial strains, makes smaller families more practical.

## RURAL BRAZIL

Brazil has a very dynamic economy, largely due to its abundance of natural resources, many of which are preserved in the largest rain forest remaining on Earth. Most of the Amazon rain forest lies in Brazil though it also extends across several other South American countries, including Venezuela, Colombia, Ecuador, Peru, and Bolivia. However, loggers are cutting that hardwood forest rapidly for farmland, for pastureland for cattle, and for timber.

The related demographic issue is that much of this land is not actually empty of human beings. Rather, indigenous peoples from many tribes live there. These Native Americans are mainly hunter-gatherers who rely on hunting game and gathering berries and other edible foods across large stretches of land. They migrate through these areas, rather than staying in fixed locations as agricultural peoples do. One of the indigenous rain forest groups is the Yanomami. According

to current estimates, only about thirty thousand Yanomami remain in an area roughly three times the size of Switzerland around Brazil's border with Venezuela. Their way of life is in serious jeopardy as they are being displaced by population pressures from outside their culture and traditional homelands. For example, about forty thousand independent gold miners have overwhelmed Yanomami territory in recent decades. The Brazilian government has worked with the Yanomami to preserve some land for indigenous peoples, much like the reservation system in the United States.

## COLOMBIA AND ARGENTINA

The fourth and fifth most populous countries in the Americas are the South American nations of Colombia and Argentina, respectively, with a combined population of about 88 million (45.7 million and 42.6 million, respectively). Both nations have very similar birth rates (17.2 and 17.1), growth rates (1.1 percent and 0.98 percent), and life expectancies (75.0

and 77.3 years). Like most Latin American countries, the birth rates and growth rates are a little higher than in North America and the life expectancies are a little lower. But these are slowly converging as birth rates in Latin America decline and economic development continues to bring greater prosperity and education to citizens.

Argentina is the second-largest country in South America by area, and it is the eighth-largest country in the world. It has a highly developed economy compared to many of its neighbors, so the standard of living is relatively high. Colombia is smaller in area but still substantial. However, its economy has been limited by a very long-running (about forty years) and low-scale but expensive civil war. As is usual on this continent, the political conflict has roots in wealth differentials and struggles over limited resources.

While Argentinian law guarantees free and universal access to contraception, the law is often ignored in this largely Catholic nation. In some cases, clinics and doctors raise hurdles, demanding that women gain spousal permission to receive contraception or needlessly referring women to other clinics for follow-up appointments. As a result, many women use abortion—which is illegal in Argentina—as a form of birth control. In fact, Argentina has one of the world's highest rates of abortion—about 40 percent of all pregnancies there terminate in abortion.

Just south of Colombia and north of Argentina is Peru. About 72 percent of Peruvian women between the ages of fifteen and forty-nine use some form of contraception. The fertility rate in Peru for this same age cohort is about 2.6 births per woman. The Peruvian government has had policies in place for reproductive health for decades. For example, oral birth control methods are available for free through public pharmacies, and abortions are legal on a limited scale.

## THE UNITED STATES AND CANADA

The United States, Canada, and Mexico are part of the North American continent. There are huge cultural and economic differences among the three nations, as well as big differences in geographic and population sizes. The population of the United States, for example, is about 317 million in 2013 while Canada's is only 35 million people.

# Easter Island

Because of their natural isolation, islands provide good examples of the effects of population pressure on limited natural resources. Easter Island is a particularly vivid example because it lost at least 80 percent of its population in just one century as population pressure ate up the island's resource base. Located in the Pacific Ocean, the island is administered by Chile in South America. Long ago, Easter Island was colonized by Polynesians, who used the timber from the island's forests to make canoes for fishing. They also farmed and built a culture estimated at about fifteen thousand people, who eventually cut down all the trees.

Archaeological research shows that the island could not support this many people. When Dutch explorer Jacob Roggeveen landed on the island in 1722, he found 887 huge stone statues that had been hewn from rock, transported miles overland, and then mounted in the ground by the ancestors of the remaining two thousand to three thousand inhabitants, who were near starvation. A century of disease and slave trade followed, reducing this native population to a historic low of 111 by 1877. One lesson: if population growth on limited land is not controlled and resources are not protected, a civilization can destroy itself. As big as Earth is, Earth is still limited. Our global civilization is facing decisions of long-term resource use (sustainability) similar to what the people of Easter Island faced a few centuries ago. How will our story end?

Canada's population density of 9 people per square mile (or 3.5 people per square kilometer) is vastly different from that of the United States, with a much denser relationship of 84 people per square mile (or 32 people per sq. km). This is very abundant living room compared to other more densely populated continents such as Asia. In addition, North America retains some very substantial natural resources of immense value, including much of the best farmland on Earth and some very large forests, especially in the northern parts of the region.

The most recent complete demographic data for the United States date to 2009. In that year, the nation had 4,263,000 births, 2,486,000 deaths, and net international migration to the United States of 855,000 people. The births minus the deaths yield a "natural increase" of 1,777,000 in 2009 (or 0.6 percent of a total US population in 2009 of 304 million people). With the inclusion of net international migrants, total growth was 2,632,000 in 2009. By dividing 2,632,000 by the total population of 304,375,000 that year, demographers arrive at a rate of population growth in 2009 of 0.9 percent. Undocumented immigrants are not usually included in such numbers.

Compared to the rest of the world, the US population growth rate of 0.9 percent is not large. In fact, it would be nearly zero if there had not been much immigration (documented and undocumented) during the last thirty years. With immigration factored in, the population growth rate in the United States has held steady at about 0.9 percent per year for quite some time. If that rate were to continue for many years, the US population would double in about seventy-eight years (70/.9 = 78).

## GOVERNMENT POLICY

Government policy in the United States in relation to reproductive health and contraception is mixed. While access to contraception is legal throughout the nation, it is not free, and individual states tend to set standards for access to contraceptive and reproductive health services. For example, no state explicitly requires parental consent or notification for contraceptive services for teens, though Texas and Utah require parental consent for contraceptive services paid for with state funds. Federal law legalized abortion in the 1970s, but since then, many states have set increasing limitations to access to safe and legal abortions.

The United States has a highly urbanized and educated female population, of which almost half are in the workforce. For these reasons, use of contraception among American women is quite high (roughly 99 percent of women aged fifteen to forty-four who have ever had sexual intercourse have used at least one contraceptive method). Of those women who use contraception, most (28 percent) opt for the pill or sterilization (27 percent), with far fewer (16 percent) relying on male condoms.

Canada has slightly lower birth and growth rates than the United States. It also has slightly higher life expectancy. And because it is a culturally and geographically attractive place to live, with ten times as many acres per person as the United States, it has a slightly higher net international migration. Long-term global warming threatens to create even more migrants from the south, looking for economic opportunities in a region with so much land, so much water, and so much wealth.

Canada has the highest life expectancy in the Western Hemisphere partly due to the country's national health-care system. Canada has lower rates of infant mortality, with 4.8 deaths per thousand live births, versus 5.9 deaths per thousand live births in the United States, and cheaper access to preventive health services.

## MEXICO

Mexico is an important bridge to the United States and Canada and to South America. Because Mexico's economy cannot support all its available workers, it has seen a substantial outflow of millions of people each year looking for jobs, mainly to the north. That surge has been reduced by increased border security between the United States and Mexico and by economic development in Mexico.

The outstanding demographic story in Mexico is a dramatic reduction in birth rates since the 1990s. In 1990 Mexican birth rates were about 30 per thousand. By 2013 the birth rate had dropped to less than 19 per thousand. That 37 percent reduction is not yet low enough for a zero population growth rate, but it is a very dramatic step in that direction. Mexico still has a pyramidal age distribution typical of growing populations. Therefore, the Mexican population will continue to grow for decades until the average age in Mexico increases, with fewer

## AHI LES VA UN SECRETO PERFECTO PARA QUE SU FAMILIA ESTE BIEN PLANEADA

Participa en la
Planeación  Familiar

FUNDACION MEXICANA PARA LA PLANEACION FAMILIAR AC

*A poster in Mexico highlights the benefits of vasectomy as a tool for effective family planning. (The red letters in the poster spell out* **vasectomía,** *the Spanish word for "vasectomy.")*

people in their prime years of fertility. At that point, birth rates and population growth may stabilize.

How did birth rates decline in a nation where the dominant faith (Catholicism) formally discourages birth control? As in Brazil, one answer is television. Starting at the beginning of the twenty-first century, some Mexican television producers started a campaign to promote birth control through very popular telenovelas. As popular actors and television personalities on these shows began to talk openly about birth control options and their benefits, the behavior of millions of Mexican women and men changed rapidly. In fact, Mexico's population growth rate decreased more than 25 percent in the first three years of the telenovela campaign (2001–2004).

Mexican workers have a very different relationship with Canada than with the United States. Canada has a guest worker program to accept Mexican immigrants. Most of these Mexican workers in Canada are documented and legal. They have a guarantee of at least six months of full-time work, during which time they make about ten times as much money or more as they would in Mexico. In addition, they receive health care. In the United States, by contrast, millions of Mexican workers in agriculture and construction are illegal and undocumented, have no guarantees of work, and receive

# Why Birth Rates Determine Life Expectancy

The connection between death rates and life expectancy is easy to understand, because everyone born eventually dies, and populations reach equilibriums. In a stable, equilibrium population that neither grows nor shrinks—and that is not complicated by migration or age distributions—death rates determine life expectancy by this formula: LE = 1000/DR. So a death rate of fourteen per thousand per year, for example, would yield a life expectancy of a little over seventy-one years. In an equilibrium scenario where birth rates equal death rates, that formula can be written as LE = 1000/BR. In this way, birth rates determine life expectancy in the long run.

This concept is very important because people around the world want to control death rates through modern medicine and effective health care. Conscious, deliberate birth control programs are generally more controversial, however. All living populations must eventually stop growing or they will destroy the environment that sustains them. But most populations want to grow until they reach the carrying capacity at which resources can effectively support the community. As a whole and in the long run, humankind must choose between high birth rates and low life expectancy (a very harsh and short life) or low birth rates and high life expectancy.

no health care. Mexican workers travel easily and safely to jobs in Canada, while many risk their lives crossing treacherous deserts and evading armed border control police to seek economic opportunities in the United States.

# CHAPTER 7
# SOLUTIONS

Never doubt that a small group of though

### sex can wait,
### but my future can't.

INTER - RELIGIOUS COUNCIL OF UGANDA

UGANDA Global Fund

## Abstain and avoid HIV/AIDS

*A poster on a busy street corner in Uganda's capital city of Kampala urges abstinence as a way to battle HIV/AIDS. The campaign, supported by religious groups, is controversial because it does no support what many experts feel is a more effective and practical strategy—condoms*

committed citizens can change the world; indeed, it's the only thing that ever has.

*—Margaret Mead, cited in 1984*

All great problems demand solutions. A variety of organizations and governments around the world work on local and global population issues in an effort to find solutions. The organizations range from local groups, such as the Population Reference Bureau and APLIC (Association for Population/Family Planning Libraries and Information Centers) International, to giant international bodies, such as the United Nations Population Fund and Planned Parenthood International, to governments and nongovernmental organizations (NGOs), such as the Worldwatch Institute. In dealing with population issues, different groups take different approaches. Some tackle physical and behavioral solutions (such as family planning and reproductive health). Others develop or implement policies. Still others promote educational programs. Some take all three approaches.

## PHYSICAL AND BEHAVIORAL SOLUTIONS

If everyone stopped having sex for about fifty years, population pressures would go away—but so would our species. Appeals to virtue have some effect, and abstinence from sex, especially before marriage, can be an excellent partial solution to population problems. Celibacy is the extreme form of abstinence, but promoting celibacy is also an example of partial policy failure. Research shows that large numbers of people do not comply with celibacy regimes even if they vow to be disciplined initially. The art of behavioral solutions is therefore often a question of finding balance between two extremes.

Birth control and family planning are areas that have tremendous efficacy in controlling population growth, partly because they appeal to more people than does celibacy. Natural family planning is another option, a method based on timing sexual activity with a woman's natural fertility cycle and other factors. However, without birth control pills or physical barriers such as condoms or diaphragms, the failure rate of this method is quite high. Therefore, safe and legal access to a variety of birth control technologies for sexually active females (hormone pills or implants, intrauterine devices, and diaphragms, among other options) and condoms or vasectomies for men is much more effective. Abortion as an enforced state policy is a radical solution that has been implemented only in China. It is not a widely accepted global solution. However, safe access to legal abortions for individuals in distress—and with various legal limitations controlling access to the procedure—is available in many other countries.

Enormous progress has been made in providing a range of birth control and family planning options for women (where options are allowed by legal and religious authorities) and a few for men. For example, condoms for men are an effective method of birth control, although some cultures shun them. So are vasectomies (surgically cutting or tying the tubes through which sperm flow to the urethra). However, on a global scale, few men choose the surgical procedure without incentives. Women in various countries, including the United States, also have access to voluntary sterilization through tubal ligation. In this procedure, a surgeon cuts and seals or ties shut the fallopian tubes through which female eggs travel to the uterus. Both vasectomy and tubal ligation are hard or impossible to reverse, however, and are therefore less popular methods of family planning.

Promoting high-quality education about sex and reproductive health has proven to be a very successful method around the world to relieve ignorance, reduce unwanted births, and to help people make wise decisions for their personal family lives and for community health in general. Safe, affordable health care is another arm in the effort to control population growth, helping to reduce maternal deaths and to reduce the rates of sexually transmitted diseases, some of which are fatal.

## POLICIES

Governments around the world have policies and laws that affect population growth. Over time and depending on demographics, many nations have promoted either high birth rates or low birth rates. For example, in many western European nations of the twenty-first century, birth control is free and sex education is part of regular education curricula. These nations remember how population pressures, among other issues, contributed to the horrors of World War II, and they work hard to avoid such conflicts in the future. Health care is generally free as well. This care, while paid for by taxes, is free upon delivery, so the cost is not a barrier for the young and the poor. As a result of these government decisions and programs, such nations tend to have low and stable growth rates and high life expectancies.

Poor nations in Africa and Asia, however, may actively resist controls on population and general reproductive health. Governments may lack funding for such programs, or cultural standards may not allow for frank discussion about sex and birth control. Some countries worry about domination by Western ideas that do not reflect local beliefs. Others, such as China, have been so strict in their efforts to reduce birth rates that different problems have resulted. These problems include large numbers of forced abortions and sterilizations, generations of single children growing up without learning the ancient virtue of sharing with community, and many more boy babies than girls. In some cultures, religion forbids women to control fertility, and it may even be dangerous for women to practice birth control. Whatever the reasons for individual concerns about reproductive issues, population pressure has become a threat to the entire living system upon which all depend, and policies are often the only realistic solution.

One of the most difficult recurring issues appears in regions dealing with ethnic conflict. There, communities may feel that having maximum numbers of children is essential for survival against rival groups. Sometimes, combatants urge women in such areas to produce as many children as possible, factoring in that some will die as soldiers. This is viewed as a way to protect the overall vitality and survival of the larger group. For this reason, efforts to reduce armed conflict can also help with the different but related goals of reducing stress on the living system.

In the United States, controversy and disagreement about abortion have led to policies that forbid US government funding of any global program that includes abortion as any part of its general family planning or reproductive health services. In practical terms, this has meant that the United States does not financially support some highly effective programs. These include the United Nations Population Fund, which helps to reduce population pressures through a wide range of health programs. These programs mainly include women's health care, education, and free or subsidized access to many birth control methods completely unrelated to abortion. However, these goals have been defunded by the United States to assure that not one penny is used to pay for abortion.

## EDUCATION

Many organizations around the world reach out to youth as part of their overall strategy in dealing with population growth. In many developing countries, young women become mothers in their teens and even as early as the age of ten. They typically continue to have children well into their thirties and forties. Such mothers often have six or more children, and in extreme cases, twenty or more. In these nations, efforts are under way to help women delay childbirth, mainly by improving access to general

*educational outreach about human* *...uction and contraception— ...ularly for women—is key to reducing ...h rates around the world. Here, ...munity health worker in Uganda ...ses anatomy, family planning, and ...ception with a young woman.*

education and by offering microloans (small loans) to encourage women to start and run their own businesses. Early pregnancy tends to interrupt education for women, leading to larger families. Extending educational and business opportunities for women, on the other hand, tends to reduce ultimate family size. By delaying childbirth, women will generally have fewer children in their lifetimes and pressure on the living system is reduced.

In the developed world, outreach to youth includes objective, science-based education in the public schools about sex and related issues. It may also include safe and affordable (or even free) access to contraception for young women and sometimes for young men. Depending on a community's standards, generalized family planning services and general reproductive health outreach to teens—such as testing for pregnancy or STDs—may also be promoted. Abortion is usually a last resort, but in some nations, access to abortion is available, especially if the pregnant female is young or has become pregnant through rape or incest. When the pregnancy is a threat to the health of the mother, abortion may also be an option. US state and federal laws, which are relatively conservative on abortion, recognize the

*Poverty and family planning collide in this photo of a man begging in front of a government poster in southern India. The poster promotes vasectomy as a quick and painless method of family planning. Effective population control campaigns around the world target men as well as women.*

importance of these complications and generally allow for legal abortion in cases of rape, incest, or serious health risk to the mother.

Education outreach to adults in the developing world includes a range of programs. These include efforts that focus on reducing the spread of STDs such as HIV/AIDS and that empower women to take control of their reproductive health for fewer overall pregnancies. Programs such as the ABC approach, which focuses on abstinence, being faithful, and condom usage, have been successful in parts of eastern Africa such as Uganda, where government support, schools, and women's groups have been key to educational outreach and the overall success of the program. Thailand, an Asian nation that has a particularly robust sex industry, was successful in requiring condom usage in brothels as part of its implementation of the ABC program.

India introduced the world's first national family planning program in 1952 and has actively promoted condom usage in the decades since then. In the early years of the program, the government distributed condoms through funding from various international organizations. As Indian manufacturers began to produce condoms, the government partnered with them to subsidize the cost of condoms. Various creative marketing campaigns followed, one of which linked popular Bollywood (Indian film) stars to certain condom brands. In another marketing effort, the BBC World Service Trust developed a condom ringtone. In general, urbanized, educated women in India are more likely to use contraception methods, while rural and/or illiterate women and sex workers are less likely to do so without educational intervention programs.

## PARTIAL SOLUTIONS

On their own, a variety of seemingly good ideas and logical projects have proven that they cannot actually solve the problem of population pressure. They cannot do so because they fail to address birth rates, which determine life expectancy in the long run of equilibrium populations. For example, increasing agricultural production alone cannot end starvation, as Norman Borlaug noted at his 1970 Nobel Prize address. Without also reducing birth rates at nearly the same time, the increased food supplies are eaten by the growing population each year.

In fact, with the world's growing population and unequal access to food, about 45 percent of all deaths of the world's children (more than three million of them under the age of five) are still a result of malnutrition.

In addition, transferring wealth from rich to poor nations alone cannot end starvation or bring an end to wars over scarce resources. Wealth transfers (of money and skills) can do enormous good through programs that help poorer countries to improve their agriculture, medicine, and general level of public health as well as to improve their education and legal systems and basic standard of living. These efforts can be very successful if population pressure is also being reduced. But if a nation's or a community's population is growing at the 3 percent rate that is typical of the fastest-growing populations in the twenty-first-century world, transfers of wealth have very little long-term impact. Donors who provide funding to such transfer-of-wealth programs want results. They may be happy to help end a famine caused by bad weather and poor harvests in one year, for example. But if the famine is linked to unaddressed population growth issues, the famine is likely to recur in a few years. In these cases, donors stop contributing to what appear to

*US president Barack Obama congratulates members of the Social Entrepreneurs of Grinnell (SEG) in 2012 for their work in supporting global microfinance projects. Originally started by students at Grinnell College in Iowa, SEG provides local and international loans to help communities in poverty start small businesses. Research shows that creating opportunities for employment and reliable income is an effective tool in population control.*

# Tragedy of the Commons

In 1968 an American ecologist named Garrett Hardin wrote a biology paper called "The Tragedy of the Commons." The main point of his paper was that if many different individuals share access to a group (or common) resource, each person will have incentives to take more than he or she might actually need, leading eventually to destruction of the common resource. Hardin's main example was the depletion of common grazing grounds of pastoral (herding) people. The concept's application to management of global fisheries, forests, and similar common resources was immediately clear to many.

The tragedy of the commons concept comes into play as leaders around the world look for effective policies to deal with population pressure and its many consequences. For example, in dealing with population control issues, policy makers have to grapple with human sexual psychology, which is generally focused on short-term self-interest. To the extent that policy makers can educate individuals to the short- and long-term benefits of practices that protect the sexual and reproductive health of the individual, long-term positive outcomes for the larger community are more likely.

be unsolvable problems until birth rates are dealt with. This is a serious problem in international philanthropy and is referred to as donor fatigue.

## PROMOTING A SUSTAINABLE FUTURE

Many excellent efforts can help solve global population pressures. For example, almost anything that helps to heal the environment helps with population pressure too. By protecting our forests, waters, and other natural resources, we ensure that our children will have access to clean water, food, and fiber without fighting over them. Almost anything that promotes peace also helps. Wars consume more resources than any other human activity. Wars also distract attention from the ultimate cause of many conflicts—population pressure leading to resource competition. Almost anything that promotes economic development helps as well, as long as this does not damage the environment that sustains us all. Almost anything that promotes human rights and freedom of women helps too. Research shows that when women are empowered to take control of their own reproductive health, family size falls. Helping men become more responsible also helps improve overall sexual and reproductive health within a community.

Almost anything that promotes sound education helps us all for similar reasons. Almost anything that promotes government transparency and a focus on the welfare of people in general instead of just the wealthiest or most powerful helps. And almost anything that helps with population planning helps, whether it is focused on the policies of nation-states or on the behavior of individuals and couples.

Young people are key to the future, and the decisions they make about family size and reproductive health matter. To help contain human population growth and to make healthy decisions for you and your family, read about the issues and learn as much as you can. Talk to people and share ideas for how you can make smart decisions for the living world. The future of our Earth and our species depends on you.

## ACTIVITIES

*You can contribute to solutions to the problems associated with overpopulation. Start by asking questions and educating yourself. Then share what you learn with others. Let them know your opinions, and ask them to help find solutions with you. Here are some ideas to get started.*

### SURVEY

Conduct a survey of your friends and classmates or of adults you know about global population. You will get the best results if you make it short. Allow people to answer either verbally right away or in writing later (set a deadline). Do a little research ahead of time so you can answer questions people might have about population issues. If you can't answer a particular question, promise to get back to the person who asked it. That way, both of you learn something. Start with three or four survey questions. If you get a lot of good feedback, you can always add more questions later.

If you are pleased with the results of your survey, you can expand it into a class report. Start by explaining the goal of the survey, and then describe the information you gained from people's answers. You might want to add some statistics to show what percentage of the survey participants felt a certain way. And you can always add images, to make it a more interesting story.

Some examples of good questions to start with are these. You can develop your own too.

1.   Earth's human population is more than 7 billion people, and it is increasing by about 80 million people per year as of 2013. What will happen to people if the human population continues to grow at this rate? What will happen to wildlife?
2.   What kind of population policy do you think the United States should have? Why?
3.   Many of the world's conflicts are related to struggles over oil, water, food, territory, and other natural resources. Do you think those wars and other conflicts can be solved without addressing population pressure? If so, how? And if not now, when?

## THE POWER OF THE WRITTEN WORD

Write a letter to the editor of your local newspaper (or papers) or to your congressional representative to express your views on population growth. Check the paper's website or the website of your local political representative to find out how to submit your letter. Most editorial pages require that letters be very short and clearly written. Politicians like short letters too.

If a newspaper does not publish your letter or if you don't hear back from your congressional representative, you can follow up online or with a phone call to learn why. Letters seldom change policies directly, but they always cause someone to think about your subject. An excellent letter in a large city paper can be read by thousands or even millions of people. And politicians are ultimately the people who make or change policies. So letters to them can be very effective.

## START A CLUB

Many schools will allow students to form clubs on topics that interest them. Ask classmates and friends if they would be interested in starting a club to discuss population issues. If they are, find out how to start the club at your school and work with club members to set an agenda. There is plenty of information about population issues on our Earth for a semester or even several years of club study.

## SOURCE NOTES

4–5    Chief Seattle, "Chief Seattle's Letter to All," 1854, translated into Chinook and reprinted in English, University of California–Northridge, accessed May 30, 2013, http://www.csun.edu/~vcpsy00h/seattle.htm.

10–11  Norman Borlaug, "The Green Revolution: Peace and Humanity," Nobel Peace Prize speech, Oslo, Norway, December 11, 1970, accessed June 8, 2013, http://www.nobelprize.org/nobel_prizes/peace/laureates/1970/borlaug-acceptance.html.

20–21  Franklin Roosevelt, "Remarks to Daughters of the American Revolution," Washington, DC, April 21, 1938, cited in *The Public Papers and Addresses of Franklin D. Roosevelt*, 1938, 259 (1941), accessed June 9, 2013, http://www.goodreads.com/quotes/tag/immigration.

23     Emma Lazarus, "New Colossus," 1883, in "What Is the Quote on the Statue of Liberty?", accessed June 9, 2013, http://www.howtallisthestatueofliberty.org/what-is-the-quote-on-the-statue-of-liberty/.

25     Shirin Ebadi, *Iran Awakening: One Woman's Journey to Reclaim Her Life and Country* (New York: Random House, 2006), 78.

28–29  *New York Times*, website introduction to Ma Jian, "China's Brutal One-Child Policy," Opinion Pages, May 21, 2013, http://www.nytimes.com/2013/05/22/opinion/chinas-brutal-one-child-policy.html?_r=0.

32     Eleanor Clift, "Asia's 163 Million Missing Girls," *Daily Beast*, October 6, 2012, http://www.thedailybeast.com/articles/2011/06/21/gender-selection-abortion-crisis-in-asia-india-u-s.html.

38–39  Marianne Gabel, quoted at *DemocraticUnderground.com*, July 3, 2013, http://www.democraticunderground.com/112748452.

46–47  Al Gore, *The Future: Six Drivers of Global Change* (New York: Random House, 2013), 372.

52     Wangari Maathai, *goodreads/Quotes*, accessed September 20, 2013, http://www.goodreads.com/author/quotes/117297.Wangari_Maathai.

54–55  Disputed attribution, cited at *Quote Investigator*, January 22, 2013, http://quoteinvestigator.com/2013/01/22/borrow-earth/.

67     Margaret Mead, quoted in Frank G. Sommers and Tana Dineed, *"Curing Nuclear Madness: A New Age Prescription for Personal Action"* (New York: Methuen Publications, 1984), 158.

# GLOSSARY

**abortion:** the premature expulsion of a fetus; a miscarriage. Abortions may be either spontaneous (naturally occurring) or induced by human action.

**age distributions:** the distribution of people in a population by age. Growing populations have spreading, or pyramidal, age distributions with more young at the base than old at the top. Stable populations have more columnar age distributions.

**birth control:** methods to regulate the number of children people produce, through the deliberate prevention of conception. Common methods include birth control pills, intrauterine devices, abstinence, and barrier methods such as diaphragms or condoms. Artificial insemination and in vitro reproduction are reverse birth control processes, increasing birth rates by medical interventions.

**birth rates:** the number of children born to a human population per one thousand members

**brain drain:** a trend in which large numbers of exceptionally educated or talented people migrate from poor to rich countries, seriously depleting the pool of talent in the poor countries

**carrying capacity:** the size of a population that could be maintained indefinitely at a given level of consumption on the existing resource base

**citizen:** a full member of a nation-state with access to all rights, privileges, and duties

**climate change:** a long-term change in weather patterns over periods of time that range from decades to millions of years

**cohort:** a group of people organized by having shared the same event within a particular time frame. Demographers rely on cohorts to organize age distributions.

**death rates:** the number of deaths per year per one thousand members of a population

**demographics:** the application of demographic (population) science to practical problems

**demographic shift:** a reduction in birth rates among young women often observed when living standards, education, and economic development go up quickly. This is sometimes called a demographic transition.

**desertification:** farmable land or pasture land that becomes desert, often due to overuse combined with drought

**doubling times:** the number of years required for a population to double at any given growth rate. The exact formula is natural log of 2 divided by the growth rate and is shorthanded mathematically as 70/GR% to get an approximate doubling time.

**ecology:** the science of interrelationships of living systems in a community of organisms interacting with their environment and one another

**emigration:** the movement of people or populations out of one country to settle permanently in another

**extinction:** the reduction in numbers of a species or a population to zero

**global warming:** the warming of Earth's climate due to increased levels of greenhouse gases, especially carbon dioxide, in the atmosphere. Most scientists believe that the burning of large amounts of fossil fuels has caused global warming. Scientists predict that global warming will bring more droughts, rising sea levels, and more extreme weather to Earth, placing increasing pressure on the planet's human population.

**immigration:** the movement of people or populations into a country of which they are not native for the purpose of permanent residence

**life expectancy:** the life span of the average member of a population derived from birth rates and death rate statistics

**limits to growth:** shortages of food, water, and other life-sustaining resources that lead, in turn, to reduced growth for any population of living things

**living system:** an organism or group of organisms, such as cells, ecosystems, and humans, with the ability to reproduce. The largest living system of which we are currently aware is called Gaia. It refers to the living system of Earth.

**migration:** the process of changing residence from one geographic or political region to another

**momentum of growth:** the process by which a rapidly growing population continues to grow even after birth rates have slowed to two children or less per couple

**net international migration:** the number of people entering a country on a long-term basis minus those who emigrate for the long term

**opportunity gradients:** variations in quality of life, most commonly in wealth or safety. Humans tend to move toward opportunity and away from dangers such as war and declining economies toward stable, peaceful areas with better economies, better education, better health care, and less danger.

**population density:** the number of people who live within a specific land area

**population growth:** the increase in the number of individuals within a given period of time

**population pressure:** incentives for people to move away from failing environments, economies, or governments due to ever-increasing numbers of people on too little land to support them well

**species:** a population whose members can mate to reproduce fertile offspring. Humans belong to one species, called *Homo sapiens.*

**total fertility rate (TFR):** an estimate of the average number of children who would be born to one woman in a population if current age-specific birth rates remained constant. A national figure of 2.1 is considered a replacement level TFR.

**tragedy of the commons:** coined by American ecologist Garrett Hardin in 1968, this phrase refers to the tendency of individuals to take more than they need of a shared resource, leading eventually to destruction of that resource

**tubal ligation:** a surgical procedure for the sterilization of women in which the fallopian tubes are clamped and blocked or severed and sealed. Either method prevents eggs from reaching the uterus for fertilization.

**vasectomy:** a surgical procedure for the sterilization of men by tying or cutting the tubes that connect sperm-producing testes with the urethra

## SELECTED BIBLIOGRAPHY

Hardin, Garrett. "The Tragedy of the Commons," in *Science*, n.s., 162, no. 3859 (December 13, 1968): 1243–1248.

Miller, James Grier. *Living Systems*. New York: McGraw-Hill, 1978.

National Intelligence Council of the Office of the Director of US National Intelligence. *Global Trends 2030: Alternative Worlds*. December 2012. http://www.dni.gov/files/documents/GlobalTrends_2030.pdf.

———. *Mapping the Global Future (Global Trends 2020)*. December 2004. http://www.dni.gov/files/documents/Global%20Trends_Mapping%20the%20Global%20Future%202020%20Project.pdf.

Salk, Jonas, and Jonathan Salk. *World Population and Human Values: A New Reality*. New York: Harper Colophon Books, 1981.

Speth, Gus, ed. *Global 2000 Report to the President*. Washington, DC: Council on Environmental Quality and the US Department of State/Government Printing Office, August 1, 1980.

*United Nations Demographic Yearbook*, 2011. Accessed 2011–2013. http://unstats.un.org/unsd/demographic/products/dyb/dyb2.htm.

US Joint Forces Command. *The Joint Operating Environment, 2010*. February 18, 2010. http://www.peakoil.net/files/JOE2010.pdf.

Weeks, John R. *Population: An Introduction to Concepts and Issues*. 3rd ed. New York: Wadsworth, 1986.

# FOR FURTHER INFORMATION

**Association for Population/Family Planning Libraries and Information Centers (APLIC) International**
http://www.aplici.org/
This website offers information from many sources around the world to help individuals and groups learn about population issues from a variety of perspectives.

Berlatsky, Noah, ed. *Population Growth.* Global Viewpoints series. Farmington Hills, MI: Greenhaven Press, 2009. This selection of essays, speeches, and government documents from a range of global sources offers contemporary perspectives on population growth, along with maps and a useful bibliography for further reading.

**CIA World Factbook**
https://www.cia.gov/library/publications/the-world-factbook/
This website provides a wealth of information about the history, people, government, economy, geography, communications, transportation, military, and transnational issues of the world's nations. It's a great site for maps, basic population statistics, and other general demographic information.

**"The Global Wombat"**
http://www.globalcommunity.org/flash/wombat.shtml
This short video, produced by the Foundation for Global Community, has attitude. It takes an amusing yet serious approach to the most important social implications of global population pressure.

**The International Planned Parenthood Federation**
http://ippf.org/
This federation of 152 member associations working in 172 countries works to provide access to family planning services and basic health care for women and infants around the globe. The website is a rich resource of articles, blogs, links, and other information related to reproductive health and global population issues.

**Population Connection**
http://www.populationconnection.org/site/PageServer
The website of this Washington, DC-based nonprofit provides daily digests of news relevant to population issues, short lists of recommended books, and a video for general education among its many other resources.

**Population Media Center**

http://www.populationmedia.org/
This group uses multimedia and entertainment formats to educate and encourage positive behavior changes. You can find some Spanish language telenovelas here, along with interviews with population experts and information about reproductive health, HIV/AIDS, women's empowerment, poverty, environmental issues, and much more.

**The Population Reference Bureau (PRB)**

http://www.prb.org/
The PRB is a nongovernmental organization that specializes in population issues. It provides a wide range of accessible global population data along with a blog, webcasts, and links to information on child marriage, girls' education, life expectancy variations among racial groups, and much more.

Poston, Dudley L., Jr., and Leon F. Bouvier. *Population and Society: An Introduction to Demography*. Cambridge: Cambridge University Press, 2010. This textbook is suitable for advanced high school students wanting to better understand basic demographics from a sociological point of view.

**The United Nations Population Fund**

http://www.unfpa.org/public/
This group seeks to deliver a world where every pregnancy is wanted, every birth is safe, and every young person's potential is fulfilled. Its more specific goals include achieving universal access to sexual and reproductive health (including family planning), promoting reproductive rights, reducing maternal mortality, and accelerating progress on UN development goals. The website has links to videos and a wide range of materials related to global population issues.

**US Census Bureau**

http://www.census.gov/compendia/statab/2012edition.html
For accurate numbers on US demographics, there is nothing better than *The Statistical Abstract of the United States*, an annual publication of the US Census Bureau.

**The Worldwatch Institute**
http://www.worldwatch.org/
The Worldwatch Institute was started in 1974 to look mainly at global soil and agriculture issues, and it remains focused on population and other big-picture issues affecting the living system of Earth. The institute's mission statement is "Through research and outreach that inspire action, the Worldwatch Institute works to accelerate the transition to a sustainable world that meets human needs. The institute's top mission objectives are universal access to renewable energy and nutritious food, expansion of environmentally sound jobs and development, transformation of cultures from consumerism to sustainability, and an early end to population growth through healthy and intentional childbearing." The institute's signature publication is an annual *State of the World* yearbook on sustainability issues.

Yaukey, David, Douglas Anderton, and Jennifer Hickes Lundquist. *Demography: The Study of Human Population.* 3rd ed. Long Grove, IL: Waveland Press, 2007. This textbook is an excellent review of the science of demography.

Yoshihara, Susan, and Douglas Sylva, eds. *Population Decline and the Remaking of Great Power Politics.* Dulles, VA: Potomac Books, 2011. This title takes on the contrary concern that recent declines in fertility, especially among Western nations and in Japan, may lead to major changes in the distribution of political and military power in the world.

# INDEX

## ABOUT THE AUTHOR

Dr. Michael Andregg has degrees in genetics, zoology, and physical anthropology from the University of California at Davis and is an instructor in the Justice and Peace Studies program at the University of St. Thomas in St. Paul, Minnesota. While teaching honors students at St. Thomas each year, he also teaches courses on green technology and on the causes of war to graduate students at the University of Minnesota. Andregg's writing credits include "The Birth of Professional Ethos: Some Comparisons among Medicine, Law and Intelligence Communities" for the *American Intelligence Journal* and a chapter on "Ethics for Intelligence Professionals" in the *Oxford Handbook for National Security Intelligence*. His book *On the Causes of War* won a National Peace Writing Award in 1999. This is Andregg's first book for young adult readers. He lives in St. Paul.

## PHOTO ACKNOWLEDGMENTS

The images in this book are used with the permission of: © Zhong Min/ChinaFotoPress/Getty Images, pp. 2–3; © Romeo Gacad/AFP/Getty Images, p. 4 (5); © The Museum of the City of New York/Art Resource, NY, p. 6; © Georg Gerster/Panos Pictures, pp. 8–9; © Paul Weinberg/Panos Pictures, pp. 10–11; © Robert T. Gilhooly/epa/CORBIS, p. 12; © Art Rickerby/Time LIfe Pictures/Getty Images, p. 14; © Laura Westlund/Independent Picture Service, pp. 7 (bottom), 16 (bottom), 18, 20–21; © David Greedy/Lonely Planet/Getty Images, p. 23; © David Pearson/Alamy, p. 26; © Richard I'Anson/Lonely Planet Images/Getty Images, pp. 28–29; © Alain Le Garsmeur/CORBIS, p. 31; © Warrick Page/Panos Pictures, pp. 34–35; © Stuart Forster/Alamy, p. 36; © Shipenkov Maxim/CORBIS, pp. 38–39; © ApelÃ¶ga/Maskot/Getty Images, p. 42; © Chryssa Panoussiadou/Panos Pictures, p. 44; © Sean Gallup/Getty Images, p. 45; © Sven Torfinn/Panos Pictures, pp. 46–47; © Art Directors & Trip/Alamy, pp. 48–49; © Megapress/Alamy, p. 51; © Wendy Stone/CORBIS, p. 53; © WIN-Initiative/Getty Images, pp. 54–55; © Eduardo Martino/Panos Pictures, pp. 57, 59 Courtesy of the National Library of Medicine, p. 63; © Everlyn Hockstein/MCT via Getty Images, p. 66; © Jake Lyell/Alamy, p. 70; © Stuart Forester/Alamy, p. 71; © Social Entrepreneurs of Grinnell, p. 72.

Front cover: NASA.

Main body text set in Janson Text LT Std 11/15.
Typeface provided by Monotype Typography.